An excerpt from this book:

"Obedience is a word that sends tremors up everyone's back. Yet obedience is the first pillar of understanding spirituality. Obedience to the light brings you power. Think of it as an opening of a doorway to greater and better things."

"I embark on this journey knowing that I am entering into fulfillment of my divine purpose. And I am obedient to my divine purpose."

"I ask you not to be fearful. I ask you to be powerful. I ask you to surrender your will to the will of God. I ask you to say:
In the name of the I AM THAT I AM,
I walk in the truth of God.
I walk in the Light of God.
I align my will with the will of God.
I am obedient to the divine will that God has given me.
I am surrendered to whatever lessons I will learn."

"Remember, for as long as human beings have their own agenda, you cannot be the empty vessels to carry God's will. To be able to carry God's will, God will have to jostle us a little bit to allow our cup be emptied. Then as empty vessels, that cup can be filled to the brim with the nectar of God. Right now the cup is half full, with doubt, mistrust, and uncertainty."

Archangel Metatron - El Shaddai

Dedicated in the name of the I AM THAT I AM

to all the Masters of Light

who have given of their Light, Healing and Protection

through the pages of this book.

And to the founding members of

The Foundation for the Attainment of God Unity

for their devoted service to the Light and the Masters.

Gifts of Practical Guidance
For Daily Living

Healing, Protection, Manifestation, Enlightenment

by Nasrin Safai
Waves of Bliss Publishing

Gifts II

Cover photo by Shabnam Sadr, Version Photography www.VersionPhotography.com.

Gifts of Practical Guidance for Daily Living: Healing, Protection, Manifestation, Enlightenment – Gifts II
ISBN: 0-9767035-1-3
Library of Congress Control Number: 2005933537

To order books from Waves of Bliss:
  Email: info@WavesOfBliss.com, Website: www.WavesOfBliss.com

Other books by Nasrin Safai
Gifts from Ascended Beings of Light: Prayers, Meditations, Mantras and Journeys for Soul Growth – Gifts I. Agapi, 2003.

Gifts from the Masters of Light: Journeys Into the Inner Realms of Consciousness – Gifts III. Waves of Bliss, 2005.

Gifts of Wisdom and Truth from the Masters of Light: Tools for Clearing, Release, Abundance and Empowerment – Gifts IV. Waves of Bliss, 2005.

Gifts From Sanat Kumara: The Planetary Logos — Gifts V. Waves of Bliss, TBA.

Altered States, Biographies & Personal Experience, Body Mind & Spirit, Chakras, Channeling, Consciousness: Awareness & Expansion, Creation Spirituality, Daily Meditation, Everyday Spirituality, God, Meditation & Prayer, New Age, Origin & Destiny of Individual Souls, Science & Religion, Spiritual Teachers, Spirituality, Self Help, The Self

STAR QUEST PUBLISHING
RENO, NV   PHOENIX, AZ
New perspectives in Unified Consciousness.
3030 E. Shangri-La Rd., Phoenix AZ 85028
info@StarQuestPublishing.com   602-482-1568
www.StarQuestPublishing.com/index.htm
Printed in Korea.

Foreword
by Dr. John Alderson, D.C.

I received a call late morning at my office from Nasrin Safai. She asked if I could assist her with her ailments resulting from extensive travels. During the course of her treatment, I had my first introduction into the world of spirituality.

Over the years Nasrin Safai has given numerous workshops all over the world. On many occasions people inquired about meditational techniques to assist in stilling the mind, raising their consciousness and reaching higher spiritual levels. These constant inquiries have lead to the writings of the *Gifts* book series. Many of us have wondered what holds us back from rapid movement toward enlightenment. *Gifts II* provides the tools we need to reach those higher levels of spiritual development. These tools are given in the four sections of healing, protection, manifestation and enlightenment. First, we have to heal ourselves from the trauma inflicted through various stages of our lives spanning from childhood through adulthood. The mental traumas and the emotional chains of old patterns slow our potential growth. The healing exercises offered in this book assist us to reclaim the power of our own divinity. Book II guides us to heal ourselves through the release of emotional fear and by infusing our lives with more love, light and joy. Next, on our journey we need to protect ourselves from negativity. Nasrin's insight and exercises help dilute low vibration, and reverse the negative flow of energy to a positive one, in the direction of light. Then, we use manifestation mantras to clear obstacles, develop new ideas, and reach new heights of accomplishments to feel the abundance of life. Through this we develop a greater ability for attaining mastery. Ultimately we start the process for our enlightenment.

John Alderson, D.C.,
October 31 2005, Houston Texas

Dr. John Alderson received his Bachelor of Science degree at St. Joseph's College in Indiana. He pursued his Doctor of Chiropractic degree and graduated from Palmer College of Chiropractic in Davenport, Iowa in 1982. Since then he has been a practicing Chiropractic physician in the United States and other parts of the world. He continued on with post graduate studies and completed two programs in chiropractic orthopedics. He also attended a three year radiology program in Dubuque, Iowa. He is a certified acupuncturist from the National and Texas College of Chiropractic. He holds an auriculotherapy certificate from the Electo Therapy Association. He has traveled the globe in pursuit of spiritual growth and enlightenment. He has visited the holy abodes of many living saints throughout the world. He has received personal blessings from Sathya Sai Baba in White Field and Putaparthi, India. He has been on tour with Ammachi throughout the United States; visited

Mother Meera in Schamburg, Germany; Self Realization Institute of Paramahamsa Yogananda in California. He has received the teachings of Karunamayi in Colorado and California. He has been to the ashram of Bhaghawan Nityananda in Ganeshpuri, India. He has received blessings from Sadananada in Bombay and stayed at the Damanhur community near Tourin, Italy. He has traveled extensively to numerous sacred sites and energy vortices around the globe.

Table of Contents

Introduction

This book has come about because of the amazing response from those of you who read my first Gifts book, *Gifts from the Ascended Beings of Light: Prayers, Mantras, Invocations, and Journeys for Soul Growth.* I am deeply amazed and forever grateful for my good fortune to be the catalyst in bringing the teachings and the wisdom presented by the Ascended Masters and the Angelic Beings of Light. People from around the world have communicated with me the lasting benefits they received from that book. The response has been so overwhelmingly positive that it has given me incentive to compile four more books in the series. In the time that has transpired since the first book, my good friend and co-traveler on the path of Light Susan and I were instructed by Metatron to begin compiling these. It might be of interest to you what the Roman numerals in the book titles really mean. Metatron explained that odd numbered books will be based on the energy of the Masters who are represented in the books. The even numbered books are based on specific themes applicable to daily life, hence the four categories of protection, healing, manifestation and enlightenment presented in this book.

My intent in compiling the information presented in this book and in book IV is to bring you practical guidance to use in your daily life. Feedback from readers of the first book confirmed the enhancement they experienced in using the exercises on a regular basis.

Ken Wilbur is believed to be the greatest contemporary philosopher of our time by scientific and mystic circles. He is a pioneer in integrating the old and the new philosophies of East and West. In *Embracing Reality: the Integral Vision of Ken Wilbur,* compiled by Brad Reynolds, Ken Wilbur states:

"The only major purpose of a book on mysticism should be to persuade the reader to engage in mystical practice." (p. 10)

The *Gifts* series is written exactly with this in mind, to give you tools to practice mysticism in your everyday life and to make it an integral part of your practical everyday living. In reading these books, you can feel the presence of the Masters and their energies through the pages. When they offer you their healing or protection, they will provide it to you for the asking. They will present themselves when you call upon them, even if you don't feel their presence. In time as you practice the exercises, you will become sensitive to their energies and will recognize their presence as they fill your environment with themselves.

Being in the presence of these highly evolved beings, or even in the environment where their energies permeates, brings us to higher levels of evolution. It purifies our own body and beingness and raises our consciousness to a higher level. It moves us to absorb more light — not just from them — but from everything, everywhere. Just like a light bulb that illuminates an entire room Being in the presence of these brightly illumined beings can shed their light upon us and illuminate us in return. The difference is that these beings have a way to transfer their higher consciousness to us and through that, raise our vibration. A light bulb cannot make us shine or see better when we leave the lighted room and enter the darkness. But the exchange with the Masters of Light does that. It strengthens our own inner light and helps us shine even when we go into darkness. It helps protect us from absorbing the darkness or pollution from the environment and gives us the inner vision and the inner light with which to choose the higher path and the brighter consciousness. It further gives us the protection and the assistance that becomes an ever-present gift from them to us. This is why the Masters of Light keep insisting that I focus my energy primarily in writing the books which permeate with their energies and spread their teachings to a much larger audience.

Books or written words carry energy. That energy becomes intensified and more potent when the consciousness of the written word, and the person or being whose words they are, is of higher elevation than our own. I do not consider myself the author of these books although I take full responsibility for my errors in omission or interpretation. This is why, as much as possible, I do not try to interpret the words of the Masters. I do give commentaries, synopses or summaries where it will help to illuminate their points. This will maintain the energy intact, fresh and original. The Masters of Light and Wisdom are the true authors, and it is their words and energies that move people.

A woman came for a private channeling session with me. Mother Mary came to give her guidance. After her reading she told me an interesting story which had led her to come for a reading. A few weeks before, I had met this woman at a week-long yoga and martial arts workshop. We had enjoyed talking to each other during the breaks, and before we parted company I gave her a copy of the first

Gifts book. She put her new book in her carry-on luggage to read on the plane ride home. While waiting at the airport, she checked her messages on her cell phone and came across a disturbing call regarding a legal matter that needed immediate attention. While she was pausing to catch her breath and decide what her next move should be, she saw the book peeking at her from her bag. She pulled it out, said a prayer and asked the Masters to give her guidance and direction regarding the matter. She paused a moment and opened the book at random to read whatever her eyes would fall upon.

The book opened in the middle of the Mother Mary chapter. As she focused on the words, she heard the words in her head being read with my voice, as though Mother Mary was talking to her in my voice. The gist of the message, as she gathered, seemed to indicate that she must not act hastily but wait for resolution, and that she must trust that Mother Mary was watching over her and everything would be alright. That gave her peace of mind and she relaxed a bit, only to last a short while before doubts set in. After all, she thought, these words were written not for divination purposes or for asking specific mundane questions but were guidance given by the Masters to heighten the states of spiritual evolution. Her heart sank again and she closed the book. Then she had the thought that, "Well, perhaps, this is a message for me right now as well as a message of guidance." She then prayed again and said, "Please give me direction again to the same effect if you are indeed talking to me about this specific problem I am facing." She stilled her mind, closed her eyes and opened the book at random again, only to find that it had opened to the same exact page again! Excited, she closed the book and asked if Mother Mary was really present and talking to her in this way, that she would show it to her one more time. She closed the book and turned it around upside down and back to the front, just to be certain. She stilled her mind and opened the book to the same exact page! Believing that this can no longer be considered a coincidence — even by her skeptical mind — she decided to do exactly as she felt guided by the words, "Wait and trust."

By the time she arrived home, there had been resolution over the legal matter. She did not have to do anything. The woman had not met me before the workshop, nor had she ever been in a channeling session. When she came for her first reading, she realized what had happened at the airport was exactly what happens in an actual channeling session; Mother Mary speaking to her using my voice and body as her channel.

Spiritual Masters are living human beings who have attained Self Realization in their present lifetime. Avatars are Masters who are born realized. Being in the physical presence of living human Avatars and Spiritual Masters is also a great and powerful tool for raising the consciousness and absorbing greater light. This is why I make a great effort to reach and inform as many people as I can when one of these beings is available on tour. When I discover a living Master and locate their whereabouts, I set out to experience their energies firsthand. Then I try to seek guidance from my guides, the Ascended Masters, to introduce them through my books, workshops, lectures, etc. As the old adage goes, "When the student is ready, the teacher will appear." We do not need to tear our hair out trying to figure out which Spiritual Master, teacher, guide or mentor we need to find next. We can simply put out the intention to receive what we need when we need it. By the grace of God and through the intercession of the Masters, we can surrender all and trust that what we need will be taken care of. Then we can continue to work our way making a difference in the world and in our own lives by serving as best we can. Through practice of the exercises and techniques, using the given tools presented in these books, we can aspire to raise our consciousness. As we move up the ladder of spiritual growth, our teachers will be guiding us through each step.

This past summer I attended a three day workshop retreat with Ammachi, a beloved Spiritual Master known as the Hugging Guru. She vibrates the energy of the Divine Mother and has her ashram (holy abode) in southern-most tip of India in Mysore. She goes on tour to America, Europe and Australia every spring and summer. To date, she has traveled around the world many times and has unconditionally and lovingly hugged and blessed millions of people. She is the 2002 recipient of the Gandhi-King humanitarian award. Her programs are free and open to all and may run from the morning to the evening, into the night and the following day. In some locations in the States, the attendance can be as many as 12,000 to 15,000 people. In India, it can go beyond 50,000. Everyone is welcome to sit in her presence before and after they receive their hug for as long as they desire. Some devotees make a point of attending more than one program and visiting two or three cities while she is touring and moving from one city to another.

Returning from one of these tours at the airport, we stopped to check our luggage at the curbside. After weighing my suitcase, the airline employee kindly said, "You are almost ten pounds overweight. If you take about five pounds out of your suitcase and put it in this plastic bag," which he promptly produced, "I will let it go through." I told him it was not a problem and reached inside my suitcase from the side to bring out the half dozen *Sacred Journey* books I had purchased at Ammachi's program in New Mexico. As I was shuffling to put down the books inside the plastic bag, a female airline employee from across the counter about ten feet away said with a booming voice, "What is that? Let me see it." I stopped in my tracks only to realize that she was referring to Ammachi's stack of books under my arm. Ammachi's energy had pulled this woman to itself through that distance. She was calling to claim another of her children to come to her. The student was ready and the teacher had staged this drama fully aware of what she was doing, using us (myself and others traveling with me) as the catalyst.

We were only too glad to share our joy of Ammachi's teaching with her. We offered her one of the books as a gift and wrote down Ammachi's website in her book so she could visit Ammachi on her next tour. As we were parting company, the woman said, "I know this is very important for me. I can't wait to go on break and start reading it. I could feel the peace coming from you even while I was listening to you talk about her."

Brad Reynolds in *Embracing Reality* states:
 "Direct approach and personal method of studying under, and sitting with, advanced teachers is a highly valued technique in the great wisdom tradition, where it's promoted as being the best way to further one's spiritual growth. This is because according to these teachings, when a person sits in the presence of more evolutionarily advanced beings, they may receive an

actual transmission of consciousness directly from the Master, often with purifying or enlightening effects. Based on his own personal experience, Wilber attests to this little known fact by explaining that "when a person is fairly enlightened, they can transmit – actually transmit – that enlightened awareness through a touch, a look, a gesture or even through the written word." (pp. 11-12)

The Masters of Light, living and Ascended alike, beckon us to ask them for help, guidance, and intercession. Lately the answer to every one of my questions of, "How can I be of service to you?" is "Pray. Pray for us. Pray for Earth Pray for humanity. Pray for God." Thinking that by prayers, they mean specific types of prayers, e.g., say the Buddhist prayers, recite the Moslem prayers, recite the Hindu prayers, say the Prayer of the Rosary, I said, "How will I make the time to do more prayers when my days are divided between compiling books and giving readings?" The answer was, "Offer everything as a prayer." Offer your day to the success of the work of the Masters. Offer the meal that you cook to the angels of light. Offer your grocery shopping for peace on Earth. Offer the drive in the car for Archangel Michael's success in removing injustice. Offer the writing of books to the Masters of Light. Offer the books you read and your readings for the success of the Master who brings the teaching. Offer your visit to family and friends for the health and wholeness and awakening of their soul. Offer your greeting with your neighbor for peace in their family. Offer the food that you eat for the end of world hunger. Offer the clothes that you wear for end to poverty. Offer brushing your teeth to cleaning the planet and all souls from pollution and removal of unclean thoughts and emotions from your body and bodies of all. Offer your shower or bath for cleansing the waters of Earth. Offer your walk around the block for health and wholeness of the living Masters. Offer your breath to God; all this is prayer."

I invite you to do the same. If this is what the Masters mean by prayer, then there is a lot that we can do to improve things without any changes in our daily routine. All we need is the presence of mind to remember offering all of our actions and to think of them as powerful prayers. I have been doing this and I find it extremely self-empowering as well as beneficial in my own life. It keeps me focused on the true reason for living this life and reminds me of the divinity within me; within all of us.

If we can remember that and believe in it and keep our focus on it, then every action becomes a prayer and every prayer becomes an event that changes our world. We have forgotten that divinity within us. As a result, we have fallen out of sync with everything from nature to each other to ourselves and to our own divine light. When we begin to pray in the way the Masters have asked us, things start to become synchronized again, and the God Presence in the form of the I AM THAT I AM begins to reach us from above, enter us and begin to act out the divinity that has been hidden within. Through the pages of this book and other books in the *Gifts* Series, you will read about the mighty Presence of the I AM THAT I AM. All things begin with the I AM and end with the I AM. This is because the I AM THAT I AM is that aspect of God which has taken form and resides in all. That is the ideal situation when complete awareness of divinity is attained. However, in the world of duality and in the density of matter the Presence of the I AM is hidden from your soul's consciousness for as long as you are unawakened to the spark of that divinity within you. When you begin to awaken to that divinity, the Presence begins to descend down to unite with your being. In the case of an enlightened soul, the Presence of the I AM THAT I AM is fully merged and in at-one-ment (atonement) with the person. This distinguishes one, who knows the spark of God within and identifies with it, from the one who does not.

This is why the Masters of Light provide us with tools for healing, protection, manifestation, and through meditations, candle grids, and mantras bring the Presence of the I AM THAT I AM closer to us. These tools will assist in receiving the Presence, to pave the way for the attainment of enlightenment. Through the pages that follow, you will call upon the Presence, feel the Presence, know the impact and experience the essence of the I AM THAT I AM as you merge and unite with it. In time, through the practices and with the guidance and Light given by the Masters of Light, an acceleration of the process can be achieved. As the old adage goes, "Practice makes perfect."

I wish you great joy and Light in the process and pray that you will use the practical guidance in your life and benefit from it in your day to day living as well as in your spiritual practices. I hold you in the Light of the I AM THAT I AM and pray for your speedy journey into the enlightened realms of God Unity.

Part One ~ Protection

Introduction to Protection and Archangel Michael

We live in a world filled with duality where darkness and light are battling for power and supremacy. Matter by its essence holds density, and density when it takes form tends to block the light and cast shadows upon us. These shadows we perceive as obstacles upon our path, in our daily life and in attaining light and freedom from obstacles in the world of form and density.

To pave the path and smooth out the bumpy road to enlightenment, we need protection. The protection can be brought to us from the realms of light by the Masters of Light. These are human souls who have graduated from living through a life filled with obstacles. They are wiser and greater than us and live in service to the Light. They may be living Masters or Ascended Masters who live in the higher realms but can reach to help us. We need protection from the darkness of the shadows and from obstacles and delays on the path of light. To succeed in attaining greater light and to move ahead in pursuit of greater wisdom, we can also call upon the angelic forces of Light. The word "angel" comes from the Greek word "angelos" which means "messenger." (Webster, p. xi)

Angels are perfect spiritual beings whose purpose is to minister, help, protect and sustain everything in God's universe. Everything, even a humble rock or a cooling breeze, has an angelic intelligence guarding it to ensure that God's will be done. Angels can be found in Judaism, Christianity, Hinduism, Islam, Zorastrianism and Tibetan Buddhism (Webster, pp. xi, xii).

The bodhisattvas of Buddhism are considered to be angels but also to be perfect human beings who postpone their own enlightenment or self-realization (nirvana, Samadhi or God Unity) in order to help others reach enlightenment. The Hindu Apsaras are angelic heavenly beings whose light brings joy, love and hope. Angels are believed to have been created on the second day of creation. The order was first light, then heaven, angels and finally Earth (Webster, p. xii).

Archangel Michael is the Angel of Protection for Earth and the remover of injustice. He is generally depicted with his sword of mercy or justice held drawn out of its sheath. He is the "Prince of Light," the "Son of Light," and an Angel of Presence. This means that he can withstand the brilliance of God's presence. He is trusted by God to spread the Light and to protect humanity from darkness and harm. Where other angels in heaven disobeyed God's command to worship humankind, Michael obeyed. According to *Encyclopedia of Angels*:

> *"Mika-El, is the angel who is obedient in his benevolence over the people and nations." (p. 366). Archangel Michael is also believed to be a "watcher" or "Grigori." Watchers were a superior order of angels whose proper place is either the third or the fifth heaven. They are said to look like human beings (except much larger), never sleep and are forever silent." (Lewis and Oliver, p. 413).*

In the first book of Enoch, Chapters 1-36, there is the prophesy of the fall of the watchers. Enoch was a great prophet of the Old Testament who was taken to the heavens above and given the tour of all the heavens because God loved him. He was instructed to write down everything he had seen to be kept as records for the future generations of humankind. Enoch was also an ancestor to Noah and lived to see Noah. Three books remain of Enoch and his visions of heavenly realms. Enoch is believed to have been taken to heaven at the end of his time upon Earth. As is stated in the book of Genesis 5:24, *"Enoch walked with God, and he was not, for God took him."* He turned into a fiery angel with 72 wings. In the book of *3 Enoch*, which was written well after Enoch's departure from Earth, it is stated that Enoch became Metatron. (Much more on Enoch in Enlightenment/Metatron section.)

In *1 Enoch*, the story of the fall of the watchers is described in detail. A group of 200 watchers, who are also known as the "Sons of God" find great attraction for the Daughters of Man and come down to Earth to pursue these beautiful creatures. Thereafter, these Sons of God mated with the Daughters of Man. Their union yielded gigantic offspring called the Nephilim. The watchers taught humankind the art of metallurgy, weaponry, textiles and dyeing, herbology, astrology, science and chemistry, as well as prayer, invocation, incantation ceremony and music and other arts. As the offspring of the watchers grew, corruption began to rule over Earth and the inhabitants of Earth began to express displeasure with the situation. The gigantic Nephilim had insatiable hunger which was exhausting the supplies of foods available on Earth. Because of their size and appetite, they needed more to eat than the Earth's humankind could provide to them. Gradually, they began to cannibalize human beings.

The pleas and prayer of the people of Earth for help was received by the great Angels of Light: Michael, Uriel, Raphael and Gabriel. They asked God to give them permission to rectify the situation and intercede on behalf of humankind. God in turn instructed Raphael to cast the fallen angels inside a hold in the desert and cover it with rocks. Gabriel was instructed to destroy the children of the watchers. The leader of these angels with his wife and children was to be bound under the rocks for seventy generations until the day of judgment. Michael was instructed to eradicate injustice from the face of the Earth (Guiley, pp. 115, 366).

This event could have been the beginning phase of Archangel Michael and his legions' work to protect humankind, destroy injustice and promote mercy. In the Christian lore, Archangel Michael is known as the Angel of Mercy. The above story distinguished these Angels of Light from the fallen angels. It can also stand as a valid affirmation in answer to the question of whether the angels ever took human embodiment. If the leader of the fallen angels with his wife and children were to remain on Earth for another 70 generations (albeit bound and locked up) then further propagation and mating of the descendants of these original angels would have caused the mixing of the blood of the angels and humankind. It also explains the passage in the book of Genesis 6:2:

"The sons of God saw that the Daughters of Man were fair and they took to wife such of them as they chose." (Lewis and Oliver, p. 413).

14

Sophie Burnham in *A Book of Angels* says of Michael:

> *"Michael is the Prince of heavenly hosts, the commander-in-chief of the celestial army. His name means "looks like God" or "who is as God." He is strong and young and handsom." (p. 107).*
>
> *"The Angels of Islam, Malaika, meaning "messengers" are guardians over mankind writing down what they do." (p. 109).*
>
> *"Mika'il (Michael) was created by Allah. He has saffron hair from his head to his feet and wings of green topaz. Each hair has a million faces. And in each face are a million eyes from which fall 70,000 tears. These become the Kerubim (cherubim) who lean down over the rain and the flowers and the tress and the fruits. Mika'il has a million tongues, each speaking a million languages." (p. 108).*

The Pope Leo XIII lived from 1810 to 1903. On one occasion, Pope Leo passed out in the middle of a sermon and was taken for dead, as there was no pulse detected on his body. He did recover to tell of a vision where darkness and evil had taken over and was attacking the church. Although he was panic stricken and dumbfounded by this frightful sight, he saw Archangel Michael who came to the rescue of the world and the church. The pope then composed this prayer to St. Michael:

> *"St. Michael, the Archangel, defend us in battle,*
> *O keep us safe from the wickedness and snares of devil,*
> *May God restrain him, we humbly pray.*
> *And do thou, O Prince of the Heavenly Host,*
> *By the power of God, cast Satan into hell,*
> *And all the evil spirits who roam around the world*
> *Seeking the ruin of souls. Amen." (Pope Leo XIII).*

This prayer is usually recited at the very end of the Prayer of Rosary as a conclusion sealing the energies in the Light and protection of Archangel Michael (see Healing/Mother Mary).

Raising the Vibration of Light

Commentary: In this meditation, Archangel Michael first leads you to form the Pillar of White Light around you. Once inside the pillar, he leads you to go to the Presence of the I AM THAT I AM, which is God who has taken form, or God in form. Every human being will ultimately know the I AM PRESENCE, which when present looks like a luminous human silhouette vibrating in Pure White Light.

The pillar or the tunnel of White Light, when called to descend, will come down from the 13th dimension of reality. In this dimension, your own Presence of the I AM THAT I AM (or God in form) resides. When you are able to move through the pillar of white light and ascend to your Presence of the I AM THAT I AM, you can have a blissful experience of oneness. In this state you will no longer feel lonely and left out. This is where you can experience your oneness with all beings and all things. The experience, even if it lasts only for a few seconds the first few times, will leave you feeling peaceful and safe.

As you practice this exercise you will be able to feel the formation of the pillar of White Light around you more strongly, and the protection of the Pure White Light will become greater. Ordinary everyday events will not affect you as much, and physical obstacles and emotional problems will not bring you down as severely any more. Once the pillar is fully formed, you are able to merge with your own luminous Presence of the I AM THAT I AM by ascending to the 13th dimension and to prolong the experience of the state of oneness. You can then begin to invite the Presence to lower itself from the 13th dimension descending down into your body. The descent will begin from your own 12th chakra which extends down inside the pillar of light to the body.

With practice, you will begin to merge with and to bring the I AM Presence to sit on top of your crown chakra (7th chakra) on top of your head. Ultimately the Presence will merge right inside the body and become one with you. At that point, you have the complete experience of oneness or God Unity. That is the state of Self Realization. As you can see, this is a process! In his zest for our greater spiritual evolution, Archangel Michael is blending all the above processes into one meditation and taking you inside the pillar of Light to the Presence of the I AM THAT I AM. Once you meet the Presence and experience the state of oneness with the God Presence, Michael immediately gives the instruction to begin inviting the Presence to descend with you back down into your crown chakra. And he does not stop there! He continues to bring down the Presence to all aspects of the self by inviting the energies from our own spirit, soul, heart and mind to join and merge with the Presence of the I AM. He then encourages you, upon re-entry in oneness with the Presence, to return to all these aspects of yourself so as to imbue all parts of your beingness with the essence of God in form.

This is a very important and powerful exercise, which can bring you the greatest protection in the Light and an experience of oneness and union with the God in form. The

Masters of Light believe that it is our divine right to merge with the Presence of God and remember our divine heritage as a spark of Light from the Heart of God. Michael is blazing the Light and pushing us forward into that divine experience. As with all things, practice makes perfect. Remember as you practice this exercise, by spreading the pillar around you and by inviting the Presence of the I AM THAT I AM, you clear and cleanse the atmosphere for higher Light to enter. You therefore will help in clearing and cleansing the vibration and the energies of the immediate environment to absorb and contain higher Light. In this way, you can benefit yourself and serve others as well as Mother Earth.

ARCHANGEL MICHAEL, CHANNELED MAY 31, 2003

My brethren of Light, I am Michael.

I offer you a procedure to raise your vibration to higher Light and to stay protected in the Pure White Light of the I AM at all times. As you evolve spiritually, you become worthy of greater light. You can conquer all obstacles placed on your path to test you. This will make you stronger in pursuit of light and wisdom. When you pass these tests, you can evolve further. The problems and obstacles serve by distracting humankind from the light, and through the distractions make you stronger and more determined to pursue Light. In the process, the more light that you hold, the greater your ability will be to cope with distractions and obstacles. The obstacles are like an egg that has gone bad. The smell and feel of it brings you down and lowers your light. When manifest, obstacles can set you back by creating chaos and confusion. To give you an overview of this exercise, I will first describe the process.

In order to change the energy in you and around you and to raise your own vibration to higher Light, call upon the pillar of Pure White Light to form around you. The Pillar of white light has its source with the Presence of the I AM THAT I AM, God in form. When you call upon the pillar of Light and enter into the Light, you move to unite with the God source whose vibration is Pure White Light. Therefore, say: *"I call upon the pillar of white Light to descend upon me and to form around me. I call upon the Presence of the I AM THAT I AM. I ask that the Presence of the I AM THAT I AM join and merge with me."*

If you have difficulty feeling a change or a shift in your own energy field, then it is important that you focus your intention and ask for the tunnel (pillar) of Light to surround you. Sometimes your vibration has stooped so low that the Presence of the I AM THAT I AM cannot reach you, because there is a certain level below which it will not extend. You have to raise your vibration to the Presence. Ask for the tunnel of Light, cylinder of Light, pillar of Light; it matters not how you say it. Once you visualize the Presence waiting for you at the other end of the tunnel and believe that it is there, let your heart convince the mind that it is there. At that point, move your energy upward. Move the energy from your heart, your spirit, your soul and your mind upward from your body out through your crown chakra. Inside this Pillar of Light, move up in the direction of higher light, chakra by chakra, to reach up to the 13th dimension of reality and meet with your Presence of the I AM THAT I AM. This is the area where your own 12th chakra is located. When you meet the Presence of the I AM, absorb, digest, merge, and unite with it. Pause and meditate for a while. Then bring down the essence of yourself mixed with the Presence of the I AM back to your heart, your mind, your spirit, your soul and into your body.

To get a much higher boost, repeat this process three times. If you wish to receive an answer, on the third repetition go up and ask your question, then stay there to receive guidance. After you are complete, return to your body and invite the I AM Presence to also return down to your body with you. The I AM Presence has been called the Magical, Luminous, Glorious, Victorious Presence.

SUMMARY OF PROCEDURES:

Sit in meditation and say the above invocation. Pause, and meditate in order to go into a higher state of consciousness. Call upon the pillar of Light and feel the descent of Light upon you. Begin by calling upon the Presence of the I AM THAT I AM and ask for the descent of the Tunnel of the Pure White Light over you. Pull your energy up from your heart, from your soul, from your spirit and mind, through your crown chakra, inside your Pillar of Light all the way up until you meet and merge with the Presence of the I AM THAT I AM. Each time you practice this you will go to a higher level until you can finally reach to where the Presence of the I AM THAT I AM resides. When you finally merge with the Presence you may request it to come back down with you into your body.

Do this three rounds: the first round you meet and merge and unite with the I AM Presence. Bring back the Presence and imbue your body with the Presence from the top of your head all the way to the bottom of your feet, all the way to the core of Mother Earth. Then you start round two:

your heart, soul, spirit and mind moving up again inside the Pillar of White Light into the Presence of the I AM THAT I AM, mixing, merging and uniting in oneness. Pull that energy vibration into your crown chakra, into every chakra of your body, down to the bottom of your feet and from your feet into the core of Mother Earth. The third time: go back up the same way, and after you have merged with the I AM Presence, ask your questions. When you are complete with your questions, to replenish your body, bring the united and merged essence of the I AM THAT I AM down into your body.

When you are in the middle of a meeting, a group conversation, with a client, a patient or child, and you feel as though your words are not penetrating or you are losing your focus, excuse yourself for a moment and compose yourself (go to the restroom if that is the only way you can have privacy). Have a precious moment of aloneness to regroup and practice the above exercises. It will take you a few minutes at first. As you practice it will become instantaneous. The Presence of the I AM THAT I AM is your divine right. The Presence of the I AM THAT I AM is the essence of the being that you will return to when you attain oneness. **The ultimate journey of God Unity is through this Presence.**

To return to God, you must first merge and unite with that aspect of God that has form, the Presence of the I AM THAT I AM. The Luminous Presence of God in form looks like a human being — it may seem to you androgynous, male or female. That is your personal individual experience. If you do not actually see the being, you may get flashes of Light or sensations in your body, calmness and peace. You may feel a warm fuzzy feeling as though you have come back to a loving home.

In the Luminous Presence of the I AM, I am your brother Michael.

Activation of the Sword of Mercy by Archangel Michael

Commentary: Archangel Michael has a sword of blue light, which holds the energy of Divine Love from the Heart of God. This Divine Love is encapsulated in Archangel Michael's Sword of Mercy. Michael and all his legions have this sword to use in defense of the Light and to protect human beings. The sword is a tool to uphold the Light and to connect God's love to the body and being of humankind.

Archangel Michael received a dispensation from God to rescue humankind from the misery of pain and suffering. This pain and suffering is the result of forgetfulness and ignorance of our own origin as the spark of God. The original plan was for Michael to activate the energies of Divine Love and the remembrance of our divinity. By pointing his Sword of Mercy at the spinal columns of his own legions of Light and the people from his own lineage, e.g. the First Ray souls. Michael awakens the spark of divinity within us through the Aquamarine Blue Ray of Divine Will of God (more on the rays in *Gifts III ~ Gifts from the Masters of Light: Journeys into the Inner Realms of Consciousness*). To accelerate all humankind, Michael later received the dispensation to bring the activation to all souls who would want it and to recalibrate to higher levels those who had already been activated.

I remember from the early 1990's witnessing group activation and recalibration of the Sword of Mercy in various group ceremonies and channeling sessions given through myself and other channels. This practice has continued over the decades. The energies of the Sword of Mercy are available to humankind for the asking. I understand that this activation is available to all first level initiates of the spiritual realms as well as to all of the higher initiates. First level initiates are the souls newly awakened to their divinity. I believe that critical mass has been achieved for this activation, and it is available on the planetary grid for all interested parties. Those who have awakened to spirituality will later become first level initiates. These will have the sword available to them by the virtue of having reached the first level of initiation. Therefore, simply ask Archangel Michael to activate the Sword of Mercy along your spinal column, and to recalibrate it to your own spiritual level of initiation.

QUAN YIN, CHANNELED FEBRUARY 13, 2004

My child of Light, I am Quan Yin.

I ask permission to invite Archangel Michael to come forth this moment and to reactivate and recalibrate the Sword of Mercy that illuminates your own body and life force. This Sword of Mercy is a symbol of Archangel Michael and the angelic legions of mercy. It sits upon your spinal column. It extends five to ten inches above the top of your head and five to ten inches below your tailbone. It vibrates a deep aquamarine blue color, especially in moments when you prepare for sending healing light and in moments when you are in deep meditation. The energy vibrates flashes of blue light. When a healing takes place, the blue light is transmitted from the healer into the bodies and beings of those who are to be healed and into the atmosphere around them. When this light is turned on, it emanates Divine Love through the Blue Sword. Then the activation of the sword brings healing to your body and your being. You can send it out to all beings — people, plants, animals — and to the five elements: Earth, Water, Fire, Air and Ether. Your innate senses know how to heal yourself in times of need, through energizing your body with the blue light. Do I have your permission to invite and invoke Archangel Michael to perform the activation and recalibration of your Sword of Mercy? If you wish to receive it, say, "*Yes*."

I call upon the presence of our Lord Archangel Michael and his consort Lady Faith, and I call upon the legions of Lord Michael and Lady Faith to take their position around the body of (*say your name*), creating a circle of light. I ask Lord Michael to stand in front of you, pointing his sword of blue flame at your heart and Lady Faith to stand behind you, pointing her sword of blue flame at the back of your heart. I ask the presence of our beloved helper Goddess Hecate to take her position with her sword of Mercy to the left of you, and I myself, Quan Yin will hold the sword of the blue flame intertwined with the flame of the Violet Transmutational Ray. And I ask Goddess Hecate to intertwine her sword of power with her Sword of Red Flame of Life Force from Mother Earth. Hecate is given Divine Power to hold the leash upon all the dark forces. I ask that she point her sword at your left shoulder. I point my Sword of Blue and Violet Flame at your right shoulder and together we will begin to transmit the energies of transmutation, power and life force. Archangel Michael and Lady Faith will begin to transmit the blue flame of protection.

You may feel a tingling sensation or heat moving up and down your body. You may see this blue light flashing; sparkles of light may begin flashing before your inner vision. At some point in this process, as the red, violet and blue illuminations of light begin to intermingle with one another, there will be an explosion of light in your heart chakra. At that moment this energy will become part of your own essence, and you will then be recalibrated to the next level of light. The Sword of Mercy will remain activated for as long as you wish. Do this exercise for 22 days, and allow your energy body to accept the vibration of the Sword of Mercy as part of its own beingness.

In gratitude to Michael and his legions, to Faith and her legions and to Goddess Hecate, I am your Mother, Quan Yin.

Rod of Power

Commentary: I first became aware of the Rod of Power when on the celebration of one Summer Solstice a group of us went to a high-powered vortex of energy in the woods of Western Massachusetts. The group that had gathered was large in number, and I was lagging behind the crowd. As I was walking and praying I became aware that the group had arrived at a circular clearing, and they were forming a circle. Ahead of me before the clearing, there were two old and large trees across from each other, giving the impression that they were guarding the gateway to the clearing. I stood admiring the two trees and said a prayer of thanksgiving for their guardianship of this sacred spot. I asked the trees permission to enter inside the sacred circle, which was on the other side of the trees.

While pausing for a response from the trees, I became aware of two angelic figures, each leaning on the trunk of one tree. Archangel Michael stood in the middle of them with a shining blue rod. He beckoned me to walk through the two trees and enter the sacred space of the clearing. As I did, I suddenly felt an electric buzz start from the base of my spine and move to the top of my head. As he was behind me, I did not have a visual perception of what had transpired. I only had the feeling of an electrical charge moving up my spine and a sudden tingling sensation in my hands and feet. This slowed me down further, and when I reached the gathering a circle had already been formed. The group members were standing in position around the circle with their eyes closed in deep meditation.

As I was positioning myself, I noticed that Archangel Michael and the two other angelic beings were going around to each individual participant. The two angels would form a triangle with each person. Archangel Michael stood behind each person holding his shining blue rod pointed just below the tailbone and sent that same electrical charge up their spine. I then noticed that everyone who had received it was emanating the same aquamarine blue-colored Light along their spines. The two angels and Michael went around the circle and initiated everyone. In my head I heard Archangel Michael say, "This is the Rod of Power. The time has come for the awakened souls to receive it at large scale. I have received the dispensation to bring it to humanity. I will come to your group and individual readings and offer it to everyone. This is an important turning point in the history of Earth. This is a moment for celebration, as great victory has been achieved for humankind."

I then witnessed councils and hierarchies of Light celebrating in the higher realms. I became filled with peace and love. The rest of the ceremony went beautifully. For a long while after that event, Archangel Michael and his helpers would appear at workshops and in group and individual reading sessions and offer everyone the Rod of Power.

Within months, I began reading about very similar initiation procedures in other channeled works in spiritual magazines and journals. In Alice Bailey's book *Initiations Human and Solar*, Master Djwal Khul explains various initiations in which the initiate receives the Rod of Power. These initiations are at the individual, planetary and solar levels, and even beyond. He describes the electrical phenomenon, a result of the initiation to the Rod of Power on Earth and higher planes. The purpose of it is to catapult the human acceleration in spiritual growth to "blaze forth" into greater Light. The awakening and stimulation of different points of Light on the human body and within the planet increases the sphere of influence of Light. It extends the Light radiance through the body of humanity, the planet and beyond. In simple terms, he is stating that the initiation to the Rod of Power increases the Light for human beings, the planet, the solar system and beyond (Bailey, pp. 94-99).

Over the years since that day, I have witnessed great changes in people, places and things from the application of the force and Light of the Rod of Power. I have also noticed that Archangel Michael and other Masters have brought variations of the Rod of Power for greater impact and for recalibration of those who have already received the original version. One variation is the Ankh of Power. This is an ankh-shaped Rod of the same blue Light which is energetically installed around the body of the recipient from behind. The loop of the ankh sits around the neck of the recipient with the cross part in front of the chest. There are many depictions of the initiation to the Rod of Power in the carvings on various walls of the temples in Egypt.

In this exercise the Aquamarine Blue Rod of Power is offered to you. Receive it with pure heart and repeat the exercise frequently, as it increases the quotient of Light that your body can receive and the electrical charge vibration that accelerates spiritual growth. If you are interested in receiving the variations and future recalibrations to the Rod and Ankh of Power, say: *"In the name of the I AM THAT I AM, I ask Archangel Michael to give me recalibrations and variations of the Rod and Ankh of Power as I grow in Light and mature to points capable of receiving and absorbing the higher initiations."*

ARCHANGEL MICHAEL, CHANNELED MAY 31, 2003

My brethren of Light, I am Archangel Michael.

I bless you with my heart and my soul. I thank you for your love and Light. I offer to you a recalibration of the Sword of Mercy and activation and illumination of the Light upon your spinal column. Those of you who give me permission for this activation and recalibration receive from me a Rod of Light in the color of fluorescent aquamarine blue. It is placed as a Rod of Light from the base of your spine (five inches below your tailbone) to the top of your head (five inches above your crown chakra). You may feel a tingling sensation in your body, most especially in your hands. This is due to the activation and recalibration of the

Rod of Power. Once it is activated, you become the beacons of Light who transmit this Light onto Earth and will anchor it through the heartcore of Mother Earth. As a web of Light it forms a grid around your individual bodies, and a greater grid forms around the entire planet.

The purpose of this Rod of Power is to activate the innate spiritual abilities that are within you as a divine being. Once awakened, you will find it easier to find and follow your path of spiritual evolution. When activated, your teachers and guides will be able to accelerate your spiritual growth and initiate you to higher levels. For those of you who are at the first level of initiation, it will move you forward to reach the second. For those on the second level, the acceleration is to the third. Those on the third level will move to levels of Mastery.

To administer the Rod of Power, I call forth the presence of Archangels Uriel and Metatron to form a triangle of Light with you. Envision yourself standing as the point of a triangle facing North. Archangel Uriel is standing behind your left shoulder and Archangel Metatron is behind your right shoulder, making the triangle complete. I, Archangel Michael, stand directly behind you. Pointing my own Rod of Power in my right hand, I illuminate your Rod of Power. An electrical charge in the color of aquamarine blue Light is transferred from my Rod of Power to the base of your spine. The blue electrical charge begins to move up your spine from your tailbone and reaches to the top of your head where the entire Rod is illuminated on your spinal column.

Pause and take a deep breath, and feel the sensation of heat or tingling moving up your spine. This electrical charge will activate all the spiritual centers on your spine and accelerate your journey on the path of Light and God Unity. Say a prayer and offer this great gift in service to the Light.

I am your brother, Michael. So it is.

Crown of Glory

Commentary: This golden crown serves two purposes. One, it activates the chakras of the crown and third eye, as well as the channeling chakra on the back of the neck, which is for the reception of verbal communication from the higher realms. Two, it protects the above chakras and keeps them connected to the higher realms. When you are able to journey into the realms of the Masters and attend the official ceremonies held in these realms, you will notice that the Masters invariably wear head-dresses and crowns of gold bedecked with gems which denote their position, title or the lineage of Light which they represent.

ARCHANGEL MICHAEL, CHANNELED MAY 31, 2003

My Brethren of Light, I am Archangel Michael.

I offer you now the Crown of Glory, a golden crown. The Crown is a connection with your own source of Light, the connection with the Godhead. Understand that your connection with the higher realms is through your third eye center and your crown chakra center. At the base of your neck below the hypothalamus, you will connect with your channeling chakra. When activated, you receive guidance in the form of verbal communication through that chakra.

The golden Crown of Glory is placed over the head, encapsulating and impacting the important chakras of the head. It sits in front of your head right over your third eye, the center for visual perception of the inner realms. The corresponding point is at the opposite end at the back of your head, where the crown sits over the back of your head. This is the center for verbal communication with the Higher Self and reception of guidance from the higher realms, or your channeling chakra. This is where you hear the words in your head, as if someone is talking to you telepathically. When the crown is placed on your head, it activates and connects you to the guides and facilitates the verbal communication in your head. The Masters call this the fourth eye.

When your visual perception is stimulated, the third eye chakra opens up and you begin to see lights and symbols. From the opening of both third eye and fourth eye centers you will begin to witness events in sequence, as though looking at an inner television screen. The Crown of Glory is made of solid 24-Karat gold. It will encompass and encapsulate your crown chakra.

The Crown of Glory also connects to the higher chakras above your head. On top of every human being's crown there is a lotus, which is the symbol of spiritual growth and the connection to higher spiritual realms. This lotus is sitting upright in the form of a bud. When the person begins their spiritual awakening, the lotus begins to open. In the case of spiritually evolved people, the lotus of the crown chakra is fully open, displaying 1000 petals. The information is received from the higher realms and transmitted to the body through this lotus.

As this lotus begins to open up from its budding phase to the fully open phase, you may feel pain on top of your head. It may feel like a band of pain. Sometimes it may feel as though the top of your head is ready to explode. This is because the energy is being poured down into the lotus to open up your higher chakras. The 24-Karat gold of the crown brings forth an encapsulated cylinder of Light, holding, protecting, loving, vibrating, refreshing and revitalizing your most important chakras: your crown, your third eye and your fourth eye. On the top of your crown, above your third eye, is a large gem. It can be ruby, emerald, sapphire, diamond, opal, orange-sapphire or a very large pearl. The gem relates to your own lineage of Light. However, to administer the full benefit of the energies, you will receive the healing qualities of all seven gems.

My promise to you is that your lives will change for the better. You will see chaos and confusion around you but you will be in peace and harmony; you will be in your own love and Light. My promise to you is that I will continue to encapsulate you in Light. Remember to call upon me on a daily basis. You have the Crown of Glory over your head protecting you from all harm in the external world, purifying your inner vision, magnifying your abilities to verbally communicate with your guides, connecting your crown chakra to the higher realms, your own Higher Self and your guides and the Masters of Light.

Call upon me. I am here at your service. I am your humble servant. I have come to rescue the Earth. You are my helpers. You hold your hands out, and your hands become my hands. I look through your eyes, and your eyes become my eyes. I speak through your mouth. I touch through your hands. I walk through your feet. Give me a chance to guide you and assist you, to walk with you and protect you.

I am your brother Michael. So it is.

Blaze Forth the Light

Commentary: Archangel Michael can send the Light on our path ahead of us and behind us, in all directions above and below, East and West, left and right, within and around. He encourages us to say this one phrase over and over again. He insists that we remember the Light with every breath.

ARCHANGEL MICHAEL, CHANNELED MAY 31, 2003

My Brethren of Light, I am Archangel Michael.

Upon awakening, call upon me, Archangel Michael, and set up this decree. First say, *"Archangel Michael, Blaze Forth the Light."* Say this seven times. The Light shall set you free from obstacles. There is only one right decision, the decision that is made to further the Light, to expand the Light, to contain the Light, to receive the Light. All of it can be done with one invocation: *"Archangel Michael, Blaze Forth the Light."*

Envision your Rod of Power activated, held in your right hand. See your Swords of Mercy illuminated. See your Golden Crown of Glory pulsating. See yourself inside the pillar of Light and say with great strength, in charge and in command, *"Archangel Michael, Blaze Forth the Light."*

33

Visualize Archangel Michael as the Angel of Light and Protection towering over you with his sword pointing to the path ahead of you. From the tip of his sword a great and powerful Light is emanating, illuminating your path. Walk on this path knowing that Michael is watching over you and walking with you. Know that Light is your guide and Michael is your helper and your protector, the most powerful protector you could ever wish for.

In the Light, I am your brother Michael.

Car Protection, Home Protection, Office Protection

Commentary: Below is an excerpt from a discourse that Archangel Michael gave at a workshop entitled Meeting Archangel Michael. I will print his exact words for its energy, and below it I will give step-by-step details of how to perform each of these protection ceremonies.

ARCHANGEL MICHAEL, CHANNELED MAY 31, 2003

My Brethren of Light, I am Archangel Michael.

When you sit in your car, call upon me to place a shield of Light around your car to protect you and your car while you are driving. When you get to your destination, call upon me to place a bubble of Light around you, around everyone and around the entire building. When you go home, call upon me to create a bubble of Light around your house. When you leave your house, call upon me to stand and hold my Sword of Mercy above my head in the center focal point, in the hotspot, at your house so that no harm in the form of energy or human trespassing may befall it. I will protect your home, your hearts, your workplace, your children and your loved ones.

Love your government officials even when you do not agree with them. Send them love. Constantly and continuously send Archangel Michael and his legions to clear and purify them of their dross so that their decisions will be for the Light and in the Light.

I am your brother Michael. So it is.

CAR PROTECTION

When you buy a car, it is very beneficial that you perform a ceremony of initiation and healing for the car and to bring Light and protection to the car through the forces of Archangel Michael and his legions.

Ceremony for Car: Bring some water and sage or incense to the car. The sage or incense carries the three elements of Fire, Air and Earth, and the Water is the fourth element. Using the four elements which are the building blocks of creation, you are increasing the potency of the healing and protection. Light the incense or sage, and go around the car clockwise from the front of the car clearing the energy all around the car. Then open all doors, and use the sage or incense to bless the interior of the car. Pour some water on each tire and say a prayer by calling Archangel Michael and his legions of angels to bring protection to you and your car. Ask for protection while you are driving the car and while it is stationary. Ask that everyone be protected from harm — yourself, everyone that drives this car and anyone that may come into contact with it.

Then stand in front of the car, and place both palms of your hands on the front hood sending the car healing and Light. If you know any healing techniques — e.g. Reiki, Magnified Healing, Healing Touch, Therapeutic Touch or any other healing modalities or techniques — use them to add greater Light and healing. Then repeat the same by standing behind the car and placing your hands on the trunk of the car.

After this, say the invocation for car protection: *"Archangel Michael above this car, Archangel Michael below this car, Archangel Michael to the left of this car, Archangel Michael to the right of this car, Archangel Michael in front of this car, Archangel Michael behind this car, Archangel Michael inside this car and all around it. Archangel Michael, blaze forth the Light."*

Say this last line seven times with force and focus, and point your hands toward the car. With this invocation you are sealing the protection and raising the Light. You can perform this ceremony when you or one of your loved ones are about to take a long driving journey. On a daily basis, you can just say the invocation for protection as you are getting into your car or as soon as you are inside of it.

An interesting story to tell in relation to car protection is when we purchased my daughter's first car. It was a second hand car which had been fully inspected by the mechanic, my daughter and her mechanically-inclined friends. We knew it was a safe and sturdy car even though it had already rendered many years of service. Once at home, together we started to do the above ceremony for the car. As my daughter was walking around the car clockwise waving the incense and then pouring the water over the tires, I placed my hands over the front hood and started sending various healing modalities and Pure White Light to the car. I noticed that there was great resistance from the car. It felt as though the car was pushing my hands away from it. I became even more determined to send it even a greater blast of Light energy and healing. The energy would brush off the body of the car and get dispersed in the air without being absorbed by the car.

This puzzled me, and I called my guides to find out what was going on. The response was that this was an old senior citizen as cars go and it was saying, "I have lived my life so far without all this Light stuff and I have done well, I do not need to go through this stuff." That made me more determined and I said, "Well, young man, you are living with us now. Whatever your previous owners did was good enough for them and for you. But in your new life with us, this is how we do it." I continued to send the car healing energy. It still refused to receive the healing. I thought that perhaps over time we could come to see eye to eye and things might change. Although I would give the car Light energy and healing whenever I rode in it (which was seldom), I did not feel good energy from the car and did not feel comfortable in it. It was, however, a very good and solid European car, and I had no rational or logical explanation about how I felt.

A few months went by. One afternoon my daughter called me and said very calmly, "Mommy, I just had a little accident. Can you please come and get me?" I smiled, shook my head and got the details of where I could find her. I got to the scene of the accident by turning out of a side road onto the main junction. There I saw my daughter's car with the front completely smashed to nothing. My body started trembling. I pushed on the brake and my car came to a halt right in the middle of the junction. As I jerked my foot off the clutch, my car died and I jumped out of the car shaking. The policeman who was directing the traffic started yelling at me, saying, "Hey, lady, get back in your car and drive on. Don't you see I have enough on my plate without you blocking the traffic even more?" I started running to him and screaming, "This is my daughter's car! What happened to her?" He tried to no avail to convince me to get back into my car. When he finally made sense of my screaming and shaking, he pointed to the curbside and I saw my daughter sitting on top of a low wall, dangling her feet in the air with a little blood on the side of her arm and a friendly housewife giving her a drink of water.

My daughter and I both survived that car accident, but her car did not. The car had made its choice not to receive the healing and protection. In the process, it had walked itself to the car graveyard, or I should say it was escorted there by the tow truck!

If you ever come across a car that has this much resistance to receiving Light and protection, use a different precaution and put a laminated picture of one or more of your favorite angelic figures or of the Masters. A picture of Archangel Michael or an Ascended Master such as Quan Yin, Mother Mary or Master Jesus will change the energy in your car, even if you put it in the glove compartment.

Another great exercise is to place a few small pieces of clear quartz, smoky quartz or rose quartz in your car to charge the car with higher vibration. Clear quartz brings in more Light.

Smoky quartz brings grounding and protection. Rose quartz brings love and calmness. Older cars are more likely to resist the Light and protection. New cars have not yet had a chance to form habits and are more accepting and receptive to energies.

Remember, everything has its own consciousness and has a life in one form or another, even manmade tools, gadgets and objects. The life force that moves through manmade and insentient things is a slower energy charge and more difficult to detect. Nevertheless, an object has a life and destiny and is entitled to some choices in the course of its life, however limited that may seem from our perspective. When you work with the consciousness of objects, you give them a chance to make better choices. If the previous owners of my daughter's car had been spiritually aware, the car's choices would have been different. Obviously it would still have died and landed in a car graveyard some day, but its ending may have been more pleasant and pleasurable for the car and for its final owner.

Sai Baba is a great living saint (avatar) who has performed amazing miracles. I had brought back from his ashram (holy abode) in India a large number of key rings, all with his picture. One went to a woman whose husband was prone to epileptic seizures. During one of his rough periods he had had a seizure while driving, lost consciousness and was involved in an accident. He walked away from the car with hardly a scratch on him, holding his key ring of Sai Baba in his hand. The car was a total loss.

The second time was two weeks later, and he was not supposed to be driving. He had a seizure, lost consciousness and had another accident. This time he did not regain consciousness so quickly. The ambulance had to be called by a neighbor, and his wife was notified to go to the hospital arriving just as they were taking him into the examination room. He had only the medallion with Sai Baba's picture in his clenched hand. The rest of the key ring along with the keys was lost in the wreckage, again a total loss. The man, once examined, had hardly any injuries at all. (If you are interested in obtaining Sai Baba's picture, go to www. saibaba.org.)

HOUSE PROTECTION

To do a full ceremony in your house and for your property for the first time, start on the outside of your house. Again, you will need sage or incense and water (you can also use dupe, Ispand, frankincense, myrrh and other sacred spices). Face North. Light your incense or sage, and pour some water on the ground. Say this invocation: *"I call upon the Angels of the North, the Heavenly gates in the North and the Masters of Light, Healing and Protection in the direction of North to protect and bless this house now and forever. I call upon Archangel Michael and his legions of Light to protect this house and property from all harm, trespassing and from lower vibrations."*

Then turn clockwise until you are facing East. Pour the water and wave your lighted incense or sage sticks in the air in the direction of East. Repeat the above invocation, and instead of North, say East. Then turn clockwise until you are facing South. Pour some water and wave your burning sage or incense stick in the air and repeat the above invocation, but instead of North say South. Then turn clockwise to face West and repeat again for the West. Use the word West instead of North and say the above invocation.

Finally, return again to the North where you started, so that you have completed the circle. There say the name of everyone that lives in the house and say: *"In the name of the I AM THAT I AM, I ask for protection, health, wholeness, prosperity, abundance, happiness, joy, laughter, harmony, right speech, right action (add whatever qualities you want to this list) for all the members of this household. I ask Archangel Michael and his legions of Light to protect everyone mentioned above and everyone that ever enters and exits this house now and forever."*

Then go inside the house. Find the point which represents to you the center of the house, or the "hotspot" as Archangel Michael calls it. Stand on that spot and say out loud with great force and focus: *"In the name of the I AM THAT I AM, I call forth Archangel Michael to stand in the center of this house with his Sword of Mercy drawn out of its sheath and held above his head."*

Envision Archangel Michael 20-40 feet tall standing in his Light and glory, holding his great sword above his head fully illuminated, vibrating aquamarine blue Light. If you cannot visualize him, then intend him to be there. Then say out loud again: *"Archangel Michael above this house, Archangel Michael below this house, Archangel Michael to the left of this house, Archangel Michael to the right of this house, Archangel Michael in front of this house, Archangel Michael behind this house, Archangel Michael within and around this house, Archangel Michael, blaze forth the Light."*

Say *"Archangel Michael, blaze forth the Light"* seven times with great strength and focus.

Then say, *"This house is sealed in the protection of Archangel Michael. I call forth the legions of Archangel Michael to take their positions standing in a circle shoulder to shoulder around this house and protecting it from all harm, lower vibrations and trespass. So it is. It is done. Amen."*

APARTMENT, CONDOMINIUM AND TOWNHOUSE PROTECTION

If you live in an apartment, condominium or townhouse where the building is not free-standing, you can do the entire procedure inside the house in the four corners. Start at whatever point is closest to North and go around clockwise to East, South, West and North again. For the inside of the property repeat all that was given for the outside. Follow this by standing in the center and calling Archangel Michael and his legions to seal the house in their protection. You may spray or sprinkle some water instead of pouring water in the four corners.

OFFICE PROTECTION

Do the same as for the house protection, only cover the four corners of your office, cubicle or desk. Envision Archangel Michael standing behind your office chair with his Sword of Mercy drawn out above your head. Ask for protection and healing as well as abundance and prosperity in everything you do and receive in your work space.

Circle of Light Space Clearing and Mantra for Protection

Commentary: This protection was given by Metatron on a few occasions, some of which had to do with young children who were uncomfortable in their bedrooms and in certain areas of their homes. The children of the New Age are all very sensitive to energies, and they feel, sense and sometimes even see what the adults are incapable of seeing.

On one occasion, I remember the mother of a 2 year old boy who called me early one morning to ask for guidance. She told me once in a while her son would refuse to sleep in his own room claiming that there were bad guys in there. Invariably when she insisted on him sleeping in his room, she would find him breaking into a very high fever and getting very sick. She had called because after her first reading with me, she herself had become a lot more sensitive to energy and was feeling something in that room. She had connected the dots and figured out that perhaps the child had a point and that the fever was his reaction to these energies.

I told her to walk to the child's room and call me with a portable phone while standing in the center of the room. We did this exercise together with me on the other side of the phone line. She felt something shift in the room but decided to stay with her son for a while longer to comfort him, as his fever was very high; he had not slept all night and was irritable and cranky. Less than fifteen minutes later, she called again to say the child was asleep in his own bed, the fever broken. I continued to see the mother at my various workshops, and all remained well with the child and with the room. She had the good sense to do a clearing in that room regularly.

Another time, I heard from a healer friend who had rented an apartment over which his new landlady and her teenage son lived. He told me that whenever the energies were a little funny and heavy, the son would act up with the mother and would get an earful's worth of telling off from his mom. Metatron's advice to my healer friend was first to perform this clearing in his own apartment and clear the energies of all unwanted lower vibrations on a regular basis.

Second, he was to befriend the teenage boy, as the boy deeply needed companionship of an older male father figure. He did both, and all was well for as long as he lived in that apartment.

It was to this same healer friend that Metatron gave the protection exercise below. It was given for two reasons. One was that the apartment was susceptible to pulling in chaotic energies to itself because of what was going on upstairs. The second was that as a healer who worked with sounds, my friend was coming across negative energy release from the body and being of his clients. These energies lingered in the apartment after the clients left. Therefore, it was important for him to do this space clearing regularly to release all unwanted and residual energies left behind, especially since this was his living space as well as his work environment. It is all the more imperative if you practice out of your home environment to be vigilant in releasing residual energies from your work space that may be lingering and attracting other lower vibrational energies.

METATRON, CHANNELED AUGUST 16, 2004

Beloved of my own heart, I am Metatron. Take a deep breath with me.

As you work with people, you need to protect yourself. For this purpose, use the Archangel Michael mantra. Say: *"In the name of the I AM THAT I AM, I call upon Archangel Michael and his legions of Light to create a circle of Light around me. I ask the legions of Michael to stand shoulder to shoulder with their Swords of Mercy drawn out of their sheaths and held above my head. All the swords touch at their points to create a dome of Light and protection over my head."*

Then face the direction of North and envision Archangel Michael and his legions in the above formation around you and say, *"In the name of the I AM THAT I AM, I call forth Archangel Michael to blaze forth the light,"* three times. Then face East and say it three times. Then face south and repeat it, turn West and repeat it, and back to North. Stand in the North where you started and complete the circle of protection by saying out loud, *"So it is. It is done. Amen."*

When you need to clear your space (your home, car, office, shop) from lower vibrational forces and energies, say: *"Archangel Michael hold your Sword of Mercy above your head and stand in the center of this room. Remove all the lower vibrational force fields, protect me from attack and protect everyone who walks into and out of this space (home, car, office, shop), for the purpose of healing from this attack."*

This is to protect yourself when you become aware of lower energies and to release them. To do this you would say, *"Archangel Michael, hold your Sword of Mercy above your head and transmute all lower forces to Light."*

Shield of Protection From Goddess Hecate

Commentary: Goddess Hecate is a great being who holds the leash over the Darkness. A very powerful figure representing the Mother aspect, she is strong and very determined in any battle and in manifestation of what she wills to bring into reality (more on Hecate in my first *Gifts* book).

HECATE, CHANNELED FEBRUARY 13, 2004

My beloved children, I am Hecate.

One very important protection tool I can give you is the Shield of Gold. I will call upon Archangel Michael on your behalf and ask him to place this Shield of Gold all around your body like a cocoon with added protection in the solar plexus. After you have received it, whenever you feel you need extra protection, call upon Archangel Michael and ask him to recalibrate your shield of protection.

Take a deep breath. I call upon the presence of Archangel Michael and Lady Faith to come forth with their Swords of Mercy and Faith. I ask Archangel Michael to place the golden Shield like a cocoon around the body of (*say your name*). The Shield is made of 24-Karat gold. It is two inches thick in the area of the heart, solar plexus, sacral plexus and root chakra, front and back and a thin Gold leaf in all other areas around the cocoon. When fully formed it looks like a crystalline golden metallic structure.

This shield has its own consciousness and can be activated upon command. I ask Archangel Michael to activate your shield and to recalibrate it according to the energy of your body. I call upon the Perfected Presence of the I AM THAT I AM and upon the Mighty Elohim Hercules and Amazon, and I ask them to guard and guide this shield of Light and to recalibrate it when necessary.

Whenever you feel the need, envision this shield and call upon Archangel Michael, Lady Faith, Hercules and Amazon, and ask for extra protection and recalibration of your shield. You can do this anywhere and at any time. Use this protection when going to crowded areas and when you feel drained. Use it whenever you feel achy from the lower energies, from the crowds or from polluted places. You feel drained because you vibrate higher Light, and crowded places are polluted. The pollution begins to lower your vibration and that drains you. When you go to crowded places, the place itself is needy of Light and so are the crowds. You are vibrating Light, and the place takes as much Light as it can from you. As a result, you get drained. The gold shield can protect you from being drained. It can also transmute the negativity from the environment. In this way you are protected, and the places you go are cleansed and cleared.

Some places of worship like churches and temples feel the same way. People come to these places not to give love but to receive it. Therefore they may drain the Light from the environment. When you go there vibrating the higher Light, the walls, the plaster, the ceiling and the windows need Light. As all things thrive on Light, they begin to pull and take some of your Light. Everything needs Light for its sustenance.

Everything has a consciousness, even buildings, structures and cars as well as trees, rocks, birds, bees and blades of grass. They have an existence, and they are giving of themselves. Think about it for a second. In their existence as brick and plaster, ceiling and walls, they are made of consciousness and in that consciousness they have choices about how and where and for what purpose they can be used. What makes one piece of wood destined to become a log in the fire and another to become a beautiful arched window in a church, a temple or any place of worship? What makes two pieces of wood from the same tree ultimately be used very differently, one built into a coffin and another built into an altar? In the same way, what makes one human being be the Light that shines upon this entire universe and another one the type that drains the Light? Pause and ponder upon the magnificence and the perfection of this imperfect world of dualities and extremes. In its imperfection, it is perfect. In its duality, it creates variety.

SUMMARY OF THE SHIELD OF PROTECTION GIVEN BY HECATE

1. Call upon Archangel Michael, Lady Faith, and the Elohim Amazon and Hercules.
2. Ask for the shield of protection to form around your body.
3. Ask Archangel Michael to activate its consciousness to go to work whenever and wherever you need protection.
4. Ask Elohim Hercules to recalibrate it as needed.
5. Visualize a greater thickness of gold around your heart, solar plexus, sacral plexus and root chakra.
6. Do this for 22 days consecutively, using the visualization.
7. After the initial 22-day period, focus on the shield when necessary for an extra boost in protection.

Cutting the Cords of Negativity

Commentary: As human beings, we interact with each other and create bonds of friendship in family and romance as well as in business and in social relationships. As part of the process, we extend energies to each other. These energies sometimes become stronger than is healthy for us, and a bond between two friends or partners becomes a controlling cord of energy exchange.

A cord is the equivalent of an energetic rope that is extended from the body of the controlling partner to the one who is being controlled. There are many levels and types of cord attachments. Two people who love each other excessively or fearfully may extend cords from their hearts to each other. Family members may extend cords of control, mistaking it for watching over each other. Lovers who have intense and controlling physical relationships send cords from the sacral plexus (reproductive and sexual energy centers) to each other. The solar plexus is the center for power. In business relationships or partnerships based on power exchanges, when cords are extended they generally go from the solar plexus (the belly area) of the person who wants to gain control to the belly of the person they want to control. The belly button is the area where by birth we are connected to our parents. While in the womb, we are controlled by the umbilical cord which feeds us and provides us with the life force. The belly remains the energetic center for the life force energy even after the umbilical cord is cut. This is the region where, as a habit formed even before birth and a consequence of a life support system, human beings connect with each other. Yet the energetic extension of the cord can become a means to control and gain power in adult life.

In many cases, the person who is sending the cord is not aware that they are doing it. They may want to win an argument, control a situation, or maybe it is simply their habit. Sometimes in intimate relationships, one partner wants the other to see things their way. Sometimes in business partnership (e.g., vendor/customer, employer/employee, seller/buyer) people want to influence the other party's decisions and inadvertently send cords to each other. All of these kinds of cords are extended from solar plexus to solar plexus. With respect to karma, they are all wrong. This is so because everyone should have the right to make their own choices, not those which are influenced by others. The example would be the car you bought because of the persuasive ways of the salesperson, or the product or service you spent money on in a shopping mall because the shopkeeper twisted your arm, only to return it later because it did not feel good once you brought it home.

Sitting in an airport one day, I suddenly felt nauseous. I looked around to see what had caused it. I noticed a woman talking on the phone a few feet away. Multitudes of cords were hanging from her solar plexus, just dangling in the air. I became curious and started to listen to the conversation. I realized she was trying to convince someone that her product was the most beneficial for the other party. The more heated the conversation became, the more vibrant the filaments of the cords became and the more my stomach churned. These bright filaments intended to persuade or control her client were dangling in the air, sending out vibrations which were adversely affecting me. Finally, I left before I became sick. Sometimes people do not realize that what they may consider skillful salesmanship is actually an intrusion upon another person's free will.

On another occasion, I was working on a project which was very important to me. I wanted it done a certain way, and the person who was doing the work for me was very disagreeable. At the eleventh hour she seemed to suddenly give in very easily, and I thought she had finally seen the light. That afternoon I spoke of the saga of my triumph while receiving a healing treatment. My friend smiled and told me that she could see the tell-tale signs of my triumph. When I asked in bewilderment, "How so?" she said that she could still see the cord that I had sent out to make sure it was done my way. The whole saga made much more sense now, especially since I had been feeling drained and out of sorts since the encounter. I asked my friend to kindly remove it, and I felt relieved and suddenly energized after cutting the cord. Persons sending a cord can often be as badly affected by their own energy drain, because energy is extending beyond where it belongs or needs to go.

The following is Metatron's response when someone asked, "Do I have the ability to cut those cords myself?"

METATRON, CHANNELED OCTOBER 13, 2004

Beloved of my own heart, I am Metatron. Take a deep breath with me.

With the help of Archangel Michael, yes, absolutely. Call upon Archangel Michael and the legions of Michael and ask him to take his Sword of Mercy and cut out all the cords of negative energy that may be extended to you by anyone and any cords of negative energy that you may have extended to anyone. Ask him to cut off anything that no longer serves you. Ask that it be cut and transmuted into Pure White Light. Then ask for the Shield of Protection to be placed around you. The shield is gold and it is like a cocoon, with extra protection in the areas where you have weaknesses. Every person has their weaknesses in a different part of the body. Some people absorb the negativity in their solar plexus, some people in their lower back, some people in the sacral plexus and some people in the area of the heart. Generally cords are extended to the solar plexus because it is the center of power. People have a tendancy to go after each other's power. If someone wants to overpower you or control you, they send you cords.

Now I ask Archangel Michael to cut all cords on your behalf. Take a deep breath and try to send the breath deeper into your belly. Move it further down your mid-section; breathe it into the core of your being. Feel it with the base of your spine, your root chakra.

Now repeat after me: "Whatever karma has caused the connection of cords between (*state your name and the name of the person*) I ask Archangel Michael to release it. I ask the karma between us be completed and concluded. I do not give permission to him/her to do this ever again."

Envision that you are being cocooned in the Shield of Protection of Archangel Michael, and in the area in front of your belly the shield is approximately two inches thick. It cocoons around your body like a gold leaf. It is as thin as paper where it is not necessary for it to be thick. But where you need extra protection (e.g. around the solar plexus, heart, sacral plexus, root chakra and around the back, the back of the heart and mid-back right behind the solar plexus and sacral plexus), it is thick. Archangel Michael and the legions of Michael will protect it and guard it for you from this day on. After you have received the Shield, you must check daily and reinforce it.

Make sure that your Shield remains intact and that there are no rips or tears in it. For as long as this Shield remains intact, nobody can penetrate it to send cords. Any negative energies that contact you will be transmuted by the Shield of Protection.

With great love, I am your father, Metatron. So it is.

Pillar of Light Protection: Release of Lifetimes of Pain

Commentary: In this discourse, Archangel Michael explains how an issue with no apparent reason for existence may make us suffer without recourse in this lifetime. These might include fear of water, confined places, heights or darkness, anger, intolerance or sensitivity in certain circumstances, anxiety or panic attacks disproportionate to the cause. Archangel Michael proposes that most likely these overreactions or sensitivities go back to traumas experienced in other lifetimes. Obviously we have no recollection of these lifetimes except for the deep scars which they have left on our psyches. These create traumas leading to overreaction and intolerance for no apparent reason in this lifetime. He therefore offers healing for removal of root cause of these traumatic experiences accumulated over many lifetimes, and he calls upon many beings of Light and healing Rays to clear these imprints. He does explain that an issue that we may have carried with us from one incarnation to another for a very long time and over many incarnations will require a longer time to release.

He compares the accumulated trauma to an onion with many layers. In order to reach to the core or heart of the onion which contains no resistance or pain, we need to remove the trauma layer by layer starting from the outermost. However, he stresses that what would take us a thousand efforts can be achieved in one try with the help of Archangel Michael, the Masters and beings that he brings to our aid. What may take us a thousand days, with their help can be accomplished in one, and what may take us a whole day will take them an hour. He also sets the healing in motion to work within us, even when we are not focused on the healing process or sitting in meditation. In using these exercises over time you may find that the same occurrences which upset you enormously before can now leave you unaffected. The fear that made you climb five stories up the stairs instead of taking the elevator has vanished and you suddenly dare to take the elevator, or the fearful plane ride becomes easy.

At first you may not even realize when, where or how the onset of clearing and relief from trauma comes about but only observe the results. The Masters work with great unconditional love and acceptance. Even if you do not give them credit for their help or do not realize that the healing has set you free because of their assistance, they will continue to help. Their intercession in these matters is to free us from pain, free Earth from dross and free the consciousness of humankind and Earth from fears, pain and pollution. They will do whatever it takes to accelerate this process on our behalf and on their own. The longer we remain in our pain, the longer they will have to stay to assist us with the release. Our release helps liberate them from their duty. They have made a point of staying around in service to the Light, for our benefit, until every soul on Earth is released from bondage and pain. Our freedom is their freedom. We all benefit from working together, they (the Masters) and we (the disciples) who are Masters-in-making.

Through this discourse, you will notice that Archangel Michael calls upon many beings of light such as Angels, Masters, Elohim, Cosmic Beings, Rays and Flames. All of these are beings and energies of higher realms which are called to our assistance. As you read more of the *Gifts* series, you will become acquainted with these beings and the energies of the higher realms and begin to build a relationship with them personally. Until that happens, be patient and trust that they are all in service to the Light and make a sacrifice of their lives, time and energy to help us go to the Light. Only beings that are highly evolved and care for others are willing to give of themselves in service to others. This is as true in our realm as it is in the higher realms of Light. In fact as we raise our consciousness to those realms of light, we will participate in these acts of service too. In the meantime, patience is a great virtue. With patience and perseverance all things are possible.

This reminds me of an anecdote. Over the decade of the 1990's in Boston, Massachusetts there was a vast construction project. It involved the building of highway systems on land and tunnels under the water which connected the city of Boston to Logan Airport, which sits on the edge of the waters of the Atlantic Ocean. The Bostonians were extremely complacent during the overly-prolonged construction project, which came to be known as the "Big Dig." To appease the drivers stalled in traffic jams, huge billboards appeared across the city reading, "Rome was not built in a day." Underneath that, in smaller letters it said, "If it were, we would hire their architects!" They were inviting Bostonians to be patient.

As you patiently read through these passages and come across beings whose names are new to you, receive them with an open heart and allow them to become your friends. I promise you will be happy with the results. Reading passages from the first *Gifts* book, Jade, a newly awakened soul from Australia, had her first feel for Metatron. She picked the passage (printed on the back cover of this book) and wrote an email to me, "Could anyone not cry their heart out when someone, whoever that being may be, loves them so much, with such generosity, humility, sincerity, patience, determination and hope? I love you, Lord Metatron, even though you are very new to me!"

ARCHANGEL MICHAEL, CHANNELED MAY 31, 2003

My brethren of Light, I am Michael.

I would like to discuss with you the healing of your bodies, your emotions and your mind. Judging by what you have been through in this lifetime, each one of you has taken on a great deal of suffering by being physically incarnate and on behalf of humanity and of Earth. There have been other lifetimes equally as hard and some even harder. The pain has impacted you physically, emotionally and mentally. In order to serve, you have to be healed and brought back to wholeness from all the suffering.

We all must return to the perfection that God intended in the original blueprint. Therefore, ask for that healing. Become aware that the healing processes can occur with our help (myself and my legions). Become aware that we can condense time and space and bring that healing to you much faster than you can bring it upon yourself — most especially if the healing relates to other lifetimes — because you are unaware of the root cause. The moment that you ask, the Gates of Heaven open up and help will come to you. Healing will pour forth, releasing all the pain from each lifetime, removing the emotional, mental and spiritual impact that has left its marks on your body, emotions, mind and soul.

Fears you may have experienced in this lifetime without apparent cause such as: fear of heights, fear of swimming or being in the water, claustrophobia, agoraphobia (and all the other phobias) are good examples of trauma from other incarnations. These traumatic experiences could be so deeply etched into your cellular and soul structures that you may still remember them even in this new lifetime. You have no known reason to be afraid of heights or water or confined places, and yet one of these or other fears may haunt you. In all these cases, call upon all the Light beings you can summon. Go into the pillar of Light invoking the Presence of the I AM THAT I AM and directly ask the Presence to support you. Say to the Presence, *"Luminous mighty Presence of the I AM THAT I AM, I ask your intercession in the matter of (state your intention)."*

Call upon the angelic realms and upon your guardian angels even if you don't know their names, and say, *"In the name of my guardian angels, in the name of Quan Yin, in the name of Michael the Archangel, in the name of the Ascended Hosts, in the name of the Brotherhoods and the Sisterhoods of the White Lodge, in the name of the Melchizedek Brotherhoods and Sisterhoods, cleanse me of my (insert your own pain or fear and its effect on your body or emotions) agoraphobia, my claustrophobia. Cleanse me of this stomach pain (name your pain), which comes and goes without any connection to what I have eaten or not eaten. Cleanse me of this forgetful mind. Cleanse me of fear of lack. Cleanse me of lack of self-worth."*

Some of these issues have been with you in many lifetimes. The onset could have etched a niche within you. Saying the invocation once is not enough to complete the process, because the mind, body and emotions will get in the way of believing that it can. Bring yourself to believe. Sometimes you do it once and one layer of the pain in released. A second time, another. These pains are like layers of an onion. Start with the outermost layer, and until you get to the core do not stop. Anger, rage, depression, sadness, grief: each one of these has its own impact on your physical body. You may not know that you are dealing with grief but you have chest pains. You may not know that you are holding onto fear but you may have kidney problems. You may not know that you are dealing with rage but you may have had your gall bladder removed or you have liver problems. Whatever the cause, you can remove the effect by invoking the Presence of the I AM THAT I AM and ask the intercession of higher beings of Light: Masters, angels, guides and guardians of Light.

You must ask first, and once you do we will continue to ask on your behalf. And every time you come back to it, we help you take another layer off and raise that vibration. We will assist with the removal of pain. Upon completion, you will be filled with Light. It will serve you to ask for the removal of fear and ask that its space be filled with Light. It has etched a groove in your psyche; as one fear is removed another comes from the atmosphere and lodges itself there. **This is why intercession of the I AM THAT I AM, the hosts, the guardians, the angels and the Ascended Beings is very important — very, very important.** *"In the name of the I AM THAT I AM, through the intercession of Archangel Michael and the Blue Flame of Mercy, through the intercession of Quan Yin and the Ray of Compassion, through the intercession of Buddha and the Ray of Non-Violence, through the intercession of Melchizedek* *and the Violet Flame, through the intercession of St Germain and the Violet Fire, through the intercession of Lady Nada and the energies of compassion and service: I ask that this pain be removed. I ask that my body, my mind, my emotions and my spirit be healed and filled with Light in all body systems, levels and dimensions of reality. I ask that they be brought back into perfection of the original blueprint as God intended."*

Write these invocations down. Keep them by your bedside. Keep a copy with you on a daily basis. After you have said them repeatedly day or night, it becomes part of your remembrance. You will find yourself saying these invocations at the moment when you need them the most.

Take a moment now to reflect on your life. Think of an issue to bring to the Presence of the I AM THAT I AM. Take a deep breath. If nothing comes to the surface immediately, then call upon Michael, call upon the I AM THAT I AM and say, *"What should I be asking for? What is the most important thing for me to be asking for?"*

And even if you already have a list, do that anyway. Once you have your list, I will do the invocation and you can make the offer. Take your time. Take deep breaths. Pause for a moment and start making a list of what you wish to release and clear. You can start with one or more. If other issues come up to the surface later, you can add them to your list as you continue with the daily clearing.

In the name of the I AM THAT I AM, God in Action, I call forth the intercession and the Presence of the cosmic Light, the cosmic beings of Light, the ascended

hosts of Light, the angels and archangels of Light, the Seven Mighty Elohim of Light. These issues are offered for clarity and cleansing through the intercession of all beloved holy and sainted beings of Light, all personal guides, and Guardian Angels. We ask for the clearing and cleansing until every individual issue is completely cleared in all times and dimensions and in all realities — probable, parallel, alternate, possible and ultimate realities. We ask that the spaces that have been freed be filled with the Luminous Presence of the I AM THAT I AM, with the Pure White Light of the I AM THAT I AM, with Presence of Light from the heartcore of the I AM THAT I AM. We ask that healing and wholeness be restored on behalf of humanity and of all souls, the souls of planets, star systems, galaxies and universes. We ask that healing be posted on the planetary grid for every soul who wishes to connect with it. We ask that a bubble of Pure White Light be placed around every individual member until each issue is fully and completely resolved. We ask for a time warp in the time-space continuum so that an acceleration of a thousand-fold be given for those issues that may take a much longer time. We ask for a speeding of a thousand-fold in time and magnitude.

That means that if you need to clear your anger to the extent of one grain of salt, a thousand equivalent will be given to you. The 999 you can use as an offering for all those who need to have their anger issues resolved. So suddenly you become a beacon of Light; you pass by people and you help them release their anger. That means if an issue was present for you for a thousand lifetimes, it will take one lifetime to clear it. If it has been with you for 1000 days, it will take one day to clear it. If it has been with you for one day, it will take one hour to clear it.

Whenever you feel an unresolved issue resurface, come back to this energy. When you have another list ready, come back to this energy, repeat these invocations and know it is already given. The thoughts have occurred to you because this is a gift from the universe. You were helped to remember to add each item to your list. Even when you are in a different time, in a different space performing a different activity, just connect with this energy, put your intention into the grid, and it will be done.

With great love, with great joy for this opportunity to serve you, I am your brother, Michael.

Vortex of Light Protection

Commentary: In this exercise, Archangel Michael teaches ways to clear your space from lingering energies. Vibrations of souls who may have left their bodies but still remain Earthbound can pollute the energy of a room, a house, a shop, building or even the air around you.

Archangel Michael gives exact instructions for setting up a vortex of Light to which we can send all these unwanted energies. The result is energetically cleaner air to breathe as well as clearer mental-emotional energies around us in our living, moving everyday environments. Any place — a hotel room you may be visiting, a shop, the local supermarket or even your favorite shoe store — may drain your life force out of you and turn an otherwise pleasant experience into an exhausting one. (There will be more information on clearing and release in *Gifts IV*.)

This is an exercise which is becoming more and more useful in the face of Earth's recent natural disasters as well as the man-made ones, in which many souls are leaving the planet suddenly and unexpectedly in a mass exodus. Usually when a soul leaves the body, there is a period of preparation where the personality prepares itself to leave the body and free the soul from the bondage of the body. This could take anywhere from a few days or weeks to a few years. In cases of sudden death, the personality has no advance warning, at least not consciously, about the soul's imminent departure from the body. Because of this, the personality may refuse to believe or accept that the body has been vacated, and it may continue to hold onto the soul, keeping the soul Earthbound. Such souls remain Earthbound and continue to act out their Earth lives. Although they are invisible to the naked eye and have no dense body of matter within which to function, they can pollute our environment energetically. Their energy continues to linger upon the land they left, the house where they lived or among their loved ones.

After the event of the tsunami in the Far East around Christmas of 2004, Lord Metatron (Enlightenment section) sent various members of our group around the world to anchor the energies of peace and release the lost souls. One member of the group who was in India at the time offered to go across the water to Sri Lanka to perform ceremonies and to anchor the energies. He reported back that the most disturbing experience was to feel the energy of all the lost souls who were continuing with make-believe versions of the story as though nothing had happened. Their sudden departure had been too much for their minds to bear. Therefore, they continued going about their Earth business as usual.

This group member contacted me to seek Metatron's advice. He asked whether he should begin to connect with these souls to convince them that they had passed and free them from the bondage of attachment to Earth. Metatron's response was that it would be too much for this member to take on such a monumental task and that it would leave him physically exhausted and energetically drained. Instead, Metatron suggested that we focus our attention on sending Archangel Michael light and on requesting that various vortices of Light be structured in different locations along the coastline for release of the souls. Metatron taught us to visualize tunnels of Light which would connect these vortices to the astral realms at different points in order to clear these realms from the lost souls and to free the souls to leave the Earthly plane.

There are times when souls linger on Earth even though their departure may not have been a sudden event. Sylvia Browne is a famous contemporary psychic and author of many books on soul communication from the afterlife. In her book entitled *Visits from Afterlife*, she speaks of the astral realms as being three feet above the ground on Earth. She believes that this is why souls from afterlife seem to be gliding in the air.

She tells the story of a physician friend who rented an office in a new building. One night when he was working late in the office, he began to smell incense and hear chimes or church bells. Then he began to see brown-robed monks gliding around saying prayers, ringing bells and burning incense. He invited Sylvia to examine the environment. Sylvia saw all of this for herself and concluded that on the site of the building there must have been a monastery or chapel for the monks. When they examined the records at the town hall, they found that indeed, there had been a monastery on that site a few hundred years ago. The personality-bound souls of the unsuspecting monks were peacefully performing their duties and their routines after so many years at the site. This goes to show that even souls who have not had a sudden departure can still remain Earthbound. These monks were only too happy to serve in their little monastery and had no desire to depart although they had left their bodies. (See Sylvia Browne's books, *"Visits From Afterlife."*)

Archangel Michael teaches us how to clear the energy from Earthbound entities. He then goes one step further to give an invocation of command for those persistent ones who may be too attached to Earth, people or places, whose energy looms malignant and causes disorder, becoming a nuisance. Although these are extreme cases, I have included the segment for your general awareness. As I have stated in Gifts *I*, Archangel Michael's sword of mercy held above his head and yours is always a sign that he will destroy any energy that may have any mal-intention toward you. Therefore, one of the best protection tools to use every day and in times of stress, fear and uncertainty is to call Archangel Michael and ask him to stand behind you and hold his sword of mercy above his head and yours, ready for battle if necessary. Remember this at all times, and all will be well.

ARCHANGEL MICHAEL, CHANNELED MAY 31, 2003

My brethren of Light, I am Michael.

In order to help free all the souls who may be suspended in the atmosphere of Earth, to send them to the Light and to release the lower vibrations from Earth, you can create a vortex of light. This vortex can be set up at a specific point when you make an agreement with me, Archangel Michael, to set it up on your behalf. We can agree on one mile North of whatever specific spot you are located at that time. Then all you need to do is call upon Archangel Michael and ask for the vortex of Light to be created in that direction. The North direction is the direction of the Gates of Heaven. It is the direction of Light. It is more effective to set up a vortex of Light in the direction of North, because the direction of North is allocated to the divine heavenly essence of all beings whereas the direction of South has been allocated to the material essence. Where North is spirit, South is matter. There is the polarity. This is why I suggest North. One mile is a safe distance. In other words, if you are in a building and you want to protect everyone inside and clear it from all negative forces, one mile is a safe distance. The intention is to clear your environment as well as to help provide an opportunity for the lower energies to return to the Light. In order to accomplish this task I propose an agreement so that vortices of Light may be created for the release of these lost souls by myself, Archangel Michael, and by my Legions, to free you from these lower vibrations and also to assist them to find their way home to the Light. If you need the vortex to cover a further distance, make it ten miles, make it 100 miles. It is an agreement between you and I, Archangel Michael, and the forces of nature. You can choose the distance to be one mile on one occasion and to be 100 miles on another if for instance you plan to be driving and wish to have protection and also to do a clearing at the same time. If you need to travel five miles or 50 miles in any direction and if you wish this vortex to be a further distance from you, you can so choose. Remember always to protect yourself with the pillar of Light. If there is an intrusion upon your energy then you will use a command to release it; you do not need to worry. You just need to remain focused. The command to depart is used in times when you feel intrusive energies around, energies that are neither welcome nor invited.

I strongly recommend that you invoke protection when you feel uninvited energy intruding upon your force field. It could happen in your car, at your workplace, in your home or in an open space even when you are going for a walk. Under any condition at all, first invoke the pillar of Light and protection around you, and then say: *"I call forth the pillar of Pure White Light of the I AM THAT I AM to form around me. In the name of the I AM THAT I AM, I command all lower energies to leave. I call forth Archangel Michael to guide you out of here. In the name of the I AM THAT I AM, I command you to leave my body. I command you to leave this room. I command you to leave this building. I command you to leave this car. I command you to leave this house."* Repeat this three to seven times in a commanding voice with force and fervor. Make it obvious that you mean it. When you clean and clear the lower vibrations you will not be drained, nor will you lose your energy or life force. You will have zest for life and feel energized.

There is no power of force higher than I AM THAT I AM. It is the presence of God in form. It is a universal sign that all beings in creation, light and dark, recognize as the supreme force. When you say, "In the name of the I AM THAT I AM," you are sending the legions of Light ahead of you, around you, above you, below you and everywhere you can imagine. All will ultimately merge and join in the Presence of the I AM THAT I AM. Our higher aspect is God in action, you and us — your helpers — the angelic beings.

Write these invocations down, and say them whenever you feel the need. After you have repeated them occasionally during the daytime or nighttime, they become part of your remembrance. You will find these invocations coming to mind at the moment you need them the most. When you remember to call for our help regularly, we will begin to appear even before you ask. Once critical mass is attained through a certain number of requests, then the problem can be released, cleared, cleansed and brought to perfection through the Light.

This is a favor to the lower energies in case they want to join and merge into the Light. Quite a few of them do because their time is very limited. Do this as a favor to the universe. You are doing this for Mother Earth and for all the souls. Your service to free them to go to Light helps Mother Earth and all the unconscious souls. You are helping to reduce the number of car accidents, conflicts and arguments. You are helping Mother Earth to clear her own atmosphere. By setting up these vortices of Light, you are inviting these beings to merge and unite into Light, where they all belong.

I will repeat again. If you are in a situation where you feel you have a need for protection as though you have been intruded upon, do this first exercise: *"In the name of the I AM THAT I AM, I command you to leave. I call upon*

Archangel Michael to set up a vortex of Light one mile North of this spot. If you so choose to join and merge into Light, you can go there. Archangel Michael will take care of you."

Then just to seal yourself, say the command: "*Archangel Michael and the legions of Michael above me, below me, in front of me, behind me, to my left, to my right, Archangel Michael within me and around me. In the name of the I AM THAT I AM, blaze forth the Light.*" Say this seven times for greater focus and greater protection. You can do this exercise every day at the moment that you awaken and begin your day with it. Begin by saying, "*I begin this day in the Light of the I AM THAT I AM.*"

Then continue with the above exercise. If you have an important day ahead of you, plan to begin a journey or have concerns and worries about how your day may go, do this entire exercise in all four directions starting with North. Face the direction of North. Hold your hand up in the direction of the Heavens above and say, "*I begin this day in the Light of the I AM THAT I AM in the North. I call the pillar of the white light around me. I command all the dark forces and lower light to leave in the name of the I AM THAT I AM. I seal myself with protection from Archangel Michael and his legions. Archangel Michael above me, Archangel Michael below me, Archangel Michael to my left, Archangel Michael to my right, Archangel Michael in front of me, Archangel Michael behind me, Archangel Michael within me and around me, blaze forth the Light.*"

Then turn to the East and say the entire exercise again using East instead of North. Then turn South and do it using South as the direction. Follow this with facing West and using West as the direction. Then turn toward the East and repeat the entire exercise using East instead of North. Then turn South and repeat using South as the direction. Follow this with facing West, using West as the direction. Finally, turn back toward the North where you started, and say whatever prayer you wish to add, e.g., *"In the name of the I AM THAT I AM, I ask that my meeting will go peacefully today."* Then end with, *"So it is. It is done. Amen."* This seals the entire invocation and encapsulates it around you.

In the Light of protection and mercy, I am your brother, Michael. So it is.

Shield of Protection of Archangels Metatron, Michael and Faith

Commentary: This is a great Shield of Protection given by Metatron. Notice that in this exercise, Metatron is asking us to call upon his/her archangelic aspect to help with the meditation. Metatron is the archangel in charge of all the Elemental beings and their entire kingdom who work with our bodies. The Elementals are little beings of light — like nature fairies and devas — who work with the bodies of people, places and things. Anything having a body is looked after by them. Metatron gives them guidance to work with healing and reconstruction of our body, its upkeep and protection.

Archangel Metatron is a great cosmic being of Light (for a more extensive description, see the Enlightenment section). Metatron calls upon Archangel Michael and Lady Faith — his female counterpart — to bring the Shield. Lady Faith and her legions hold the qualities of faith and administer those qualities to humankind upon asking. Archangel Michael and his legions hold the qualities of mercy and protection and are here on Earth to protect humankind with their mercy. One of these tools is the Shield which Archangel Metatron is inviting Michael and Faith to give you.

If you wish to receive Archangel Michael's Shield of Protection, say the following out loud or quietly with clear mind and sincere heart: *"I call upon Archangel Metatron and all the elementals who are responsible for my health, wholeness and wellbeing. I wish to receive the Shield of Protection. I call upon the presence of Archangel Michael and the legions of Michael with their swords of mercy drawn out. I call upon the presence of Lady Faith, Archangel Michael's consort, and the legions of Faith, and I ask that they draw out their Swords of Faith and Mercy. I give permission for the Shield of Protection to be placed around my body and to protect me from all harm and lower energies."*

METATRON, CHANNELED AUGUST 17, 2004

Beloved of my own heart, I am Metatron. Take a deep breath with me.

Envision yourself standing in the center of a triangle with Archangel Michael in front of you to your left, Archangel Lady Faith is in front of you to the right and Archangel Metatron is behind you. Lady Faith's legions of faith and Archangel Michael's legions of mercy create two circles of Light around you. The legions of Faith create an inner circle and the legions of Michael create an outer circle. A bubble of Light protection is created all around you. The swords of both legions are drawn out of their sheaths and held up above their heads in the air. The swords are drawn, and the legions are creating an entire circle around you. Envision yourself standing with the tips of the Swords of Faith and Mercy pointing above your head. From touching the swords of Faith and Mercy together, a light activation takes place. An emanation of blue light pours down creating a huge blue cocoon of light around you.

Archangel Michael will now administer his Shield of Protection around your body. The Shield of Protection forms a cocoon around your body. In the areas where you need the most protection — specifically in front of the solar plexus where the power center is located — the thickness can be up to two inches. This shield will protect you from lower vibrations and will transmute them on contact. It will not affect any higher vibration; it will be receptive to transmit the higher vibration to you. It will protect you from any pain. If you are touching or healing others, it will not allow negative energy to penetrate your body or auric field. It will protect you from lower vibration and attack from any negative energies or thoughtforms yours or others, provided you are willing to let go of them. The shield will absorb and transmute all negativity. If anyone sends you negative thoughts, the shield will prevent their contact with you. Upon contact with this shield, all negative energies and thoughtforms sent to you will be transmuted and turned into Pure White Light.

Very clearly envision the shield around your entire body now. If you are unable to visualize it, then intend it to be there. Feel the thickness. It vibrates pure 24-Karat gold. Twenty-four Karat gold has extremely powerful transmutational qualities. It cleans your physical body of all negativity that causes pain. It cleans the emotional body from negative emotions and thoughts. In the areas where you have vulnerable spots the shield is very thick; two to three inches thick twenty-four Karat liquid gold. You may have a tingling sensation, coolness or warmth all over your body. It may feel as gold feels to the touch.

This shield has its own consciousness. It can bring you protection and allow all the good things and the higher vibrations to come into your body. It will not interfere with anything of higher vibration of Light. It will only intercede on your behalf and prevent the negativity and lower vibration to be released and transmuted. It will transmute all lower vibrations, anything that may lead to sickness and what might inflict or impose pain upon your body and your being, your mind, emotions and spirit as well as transmuting all pollution. It will prevent energetic pollution from penetrating into your body.

Every day as you awaken, envision your Shield of Protection around you like a shimmering cocoon of liquid light. Tell your mind that nothing can penetrate this shield. Whenever you find yourself in difficult situations, call the Shield of Protection by visualizing it around your body and command protection from Archangels Metatron, Michael and Faith. If you have difficulty commanding, then request it. Commands are more effective because they place you in a position of power. Do the visualization for 22 days. After that, it should become part of your energy body. You master anything that you do for 22 consecutive days without any breaks. Twenty-two is the number for Mastery. Your body and being should automatically form the shield around you after this period of time. You can always call a reinforcement of the shield when you need extra protection, when you feel anxious, out of sorts or ungrounded.

With great love, I am your father, Metatron.

SUMMARY OF THE SHIELD OF PROTECTION MEDITATION PROCEDURE

1. Call upon Archangels Metatron, Michael and Faith.
2. Envision standing in the center of a triangle with Faith and Michael as two points of the triangle in front of you and Archangel Metatron as the third point behind you.
3. Envision the legions of Faith in a circle around you with the swords of faith drawn out of their sheaths held over their heads with the tips touching.
4. Envision the legions of Michael standing in a circle shoulder to shoulder around the legions of Faith with their swords of mercy held out, touching the swords of faith from above, creating a dome of light and protection above your head.
5. Envision the blue light of Divine Love emanating from the swords, showering down over your body from the touch of all the swords of faith and mercy.
6. Call upon Archangel Michael to form the golden Shield of Protection around your body.
7. Visualize your body cocooned inside the 24-Karat gold shield.
8. In the area of the solar plexus the shield is much thicker.
9. Hold this vision long enough to feel it around you.
10. Every morning for the first 22 days follow the above procedure. You may notice after a few repetitions that the shield is already there when you begin the meditation. In that case, you only need to spend a minute

to check on it and make sure it covers your entire body.

11. Every morning upon awakening, reinforce by visualizing the cocoon of the Shield of Protection fully formed around you.

12. At times when you feel the need for extra protection, take a moment and do the entire procedure step by step. You may only need to focus on it for a second before it automatically forms around your body.

Quan Yin's Strength and Protection Grid With Archangels Uriel, Metatron, Michael and Raphael

QUAN YIN, CHANNELED JULY 18, 2005

My children of Light, I am Quan Yin.

I am going to offer you a gift. This is for strength and protection. It will make you strong in coping with the negative energies which cause people to behave in selfish ways, in unpredictable ways, in self-centered ways. (Note: Energies are coming to Earth which are pushing people to release their negative emotions. As a result, those emotions are expressed as people bring them to the surface in order to release them from their beingness.)

Take a deep breath. Hold your focus in your solar plexus. Still the mind and feel my presence. Feel the sensation of a pulse moving in your solar plexus, around your belly button. It may take a couple of minutes. Take your time, breathe into it and feel the pulse. Gradually I will increase this pulse.

Now envision a lotus flower, wide open in the color of yellow that sits right behind your belly button. In this lotus flower, I will place the qualities and the power of protection and strength, fearlessness, ability to cope and detachment from all negative emotions. You will not feel lonely or unjustified. You may be the only one who can think according to the universal Laws of Divine Love. **Lack of support from others does not make you wrong.** You have to uphold the Light, and you will. The time will come very soon where you will no longer be in minority. This lotus flower is very strong. It strengthens your power center which resides around your belly button. It gives you protection from all harm and releases you from all uncertainties.

I now call forth the Archangels of Light to come to your guidance and your assistance. Focus on each of these Archangelic forces as I call upon them. From this point on, focus also on the lotus in your solar plexus daily. You must awaken every morning and exercise this energy around your body and call upon the four Archangelic forces to protect you. Every night before you fall asleep, call the four Archangelic forces to guide you and protect you in dreamtime and to take you to the higher dimensions to teach you how to cope with this mundane reality. Keep your focus on this meditation while I help you form the energy grid of protection around you.

Now, focus on the pulse in the center of your belly. The rhythm of the pulse in your belly makes the lotus flower send energy from its center to your belly button. When you experience the rhythm of that pulse and you can see the golden yellow light emanating from the lotus flower, I will call the four Archangelic forces one by one for your strength and protection. Pause here and feel the pulse in your belly first.

I, Quan Yin, call upon Archangel Uriel, the Angel of Inner Light, to come forth and hold her position in the direction of North, above (*say your name*)'s head. Holding this vortex of light open and illuminated, Uriel will begin sending strength, stamina, life force, courage, righteousness, truth, compassion and kindness to your body and beingness. Golden white light emanates from the body and beingness of Uriel, penetrating, guiding, protecting and guarding your five body systems: the physical body, etheric body, emotional body, mental body and the spiritual body.

I now call forth your aspects of personality, soul and spirit to come forward and merge, uniting in the Light of Uriel. Feel your body completely filled with the golden yellow. Feel Uriel's presence hovering above your head, sending energy showers of Light to your own body. Pause and sit still, receiving Archangel Uriel's energy.

I, Quan Yin, now call forth the energy vibration of Archangel Metatron to come forth and hold his position in the direction of South. From down below, pulling the energies of Mother Earth, helping you to be grounded with, connected to, and strengthened by the energy vibration of Earth and nature, receiving nourishment from Earth. I ask Archangel Metatron to help your body and beingness cope with being in physical embodiment and with this physical density which is beyond the comprehension of your soul, for your soul is pure and does not entertain negative emotions.

I ask in the name of the I AM THAT I AM that Archangel Metaron bring the qualities of acceptance and surrender to the Light and detachment from lower vibrations and negative emotions to (*say your name*). I ask Archangel Metatron to bring forth the pure light of the red life force energies from the Earth and administer it to you. Especially in the area of the solar plexus, protecting you and connecting to Earth and natural forces, helping you to cope with Earthly and natural events and with circumstances of life on Earth.

Pause for a moment and feel your solar plexus warming up with the life force energy moving from the bottom of your feet up into your ankles, your knees, your thighs, your hips, through your root chakra, your sacral plexus and into your solar plexus. Coming to your diaphragm is this beautiful blood red, pure light energy. Feel the pulse of your solar plexus in rhythm with this red life force. Sit with this energy and with the presence of Metatron for a moment.

Take a deep breath. I call forth the energies of Archangel Michael to come forth and hold position in the direction of East, to the right of you. He is bringing the quality of Divine Power in the emanation of the blue light, the Will of God to your solar plexus. Envision deep blue light emanating from the heart and beingness of Archangel Michael as he takes his position on your right. Receive the blue light directly in your solar plexus and feel the warmth of the divine power: power to serve the Light, power to know the God within you and the God above you as one, power to realize that you can be the catalyst to remind those who have forgotten their divinity.

I ask Archangel Michael to guide you and protect you at all times and to be a constant reminder that the Divine Will of God is emanating inside the core of your own being in your solar plexus. This Divine Will is your guiding force. It will bring you greater will to accomplish your mission and your vocation, greater will to love people in spite of their shortcomings and to not be deterred by their insecurities but become instead more determined to help them rise above their own ignorance and forgetfulness. This light of Divine Will gives you strength to become the catalyst to remind others of their own divinity. Feel the blue light inside your belly. Feel the warmth and the power emanate through your body. Feel that strength move through your veins and empower you. Sit in this rhythmic pulse and pause.

Take a deep breath. I call forth the presence of Archangel Raphael, the Angel of Healing and Ministration, emanating the golden pink Ray of Divine Love of God. Directing energy to your solar plexus, Raphael takes her position to your left in the direction of West. Pink and gold rays are received by your solar plexus to strengthen you first and foremost in the love of the Self. The love of the God within you will help you to stand in Truth and to not waver from it, to not bend the rules for success but rather to succeed in spite of all odds. For **the power of love is the greatest power in all the universe and beyond**. Golden pink light of Divine Love is emanating from the heart and beingness of Archangel Raphael, bringing great healing, joy, satisfaction, contentment, acceptance and surrender to your body, the mind, emotions, soul and spirit. Sit and bathe in this energy. Feel the warmth of Divine Love spread itself into your veins through your solar plexus. Breathe in this love and let it move to every cell, every molecule, every atom, every iota and every electron of your being.

In the name of the I AM THAT I AM, I, Quan Yin, ask for a complete healing for (*say your name*). I ask for permission to restore Divine Power, strength and stamina, ability to cope with physical mundane reality and remembrance of the Divine Spark within your heart. In the name of the I AM THAT I AM, I, Quan Yin, intercede on your behalf and ask for total surrender to the Light and acceptance of her/his own mission as a Divine Spark of God — a Divine Spark amidst and amongst souls who have forgotten, souls who are choosing ignorance as their excuse to abuse, disregard, ignore or disrespect other souls.

I ask in the name of the I AM THAT I AM on your behalf that you be given the ability to rise above the negative emotions and expressions of this mundane reality and to constantly hold your thoughts and your actions on the higher Light, the Divine Spark that illumines your own heart, mind, body, emotions, soul and spirit. I ask that you be reminded of that same illumination in the hearts, mind, bodies, emotions, souls and spirits of all people. I ask in the name of the I AM THAT I AM through the healing energies of Uriel, Metatron, Michael and Raphael that energies of the Divine Spark shall fully establish a connection to Earth and nature and that the divine power and the divine love be fully established in your body and beingness from this day forward. I ask that this grid of light be established around your body and beingness and continue its work throughout your life in this embodiment. I ask this in the name of the I AM THAT I AM through the intercession of all the Buddhas and Bodhisattvas of compassion and through the protection of the Seven Mighty Elohim of Light. Do this meditation twice a day for 22 days.

With great love, I am your mother, Quan Yin. So it is. It is done. Amen.

Quan Yin's Invocation for Help and Healing in Times of Emergency

QUAN YIN, CHANNELED SPRING 1997

My children of Light, I am Quan Yin.

Let us set the intention in times of emergencies — whenever you are in need — that help be given from the higher realms. Even when you forget to call upon your angels of protection, your guides, the Masters and helpers that the call will automatically be sent out on your behalf from this day forward.

In the name of the I AM THAT I AM by the creative powers of this universe, I (say your name), request the Presence of the Assembly of the Cosmic Beings of Light, the Ascended Masters of Light, the Hierarchies of Sisterhood and Brotherhood of the White Lodge, the Orders of Melchizedek, the Orders of the Dolphins and Whales, my own Higher Self I AM Presence and my Godself. I call them forth to be present in all events, all situations and circumstances where I need their help, most especially in times of emergency. I request that immediate help be given to me in all times of need.

By extending this intention and request now, I will receive help from all the realms of Light, in all moments, in all dimensions and realities, in all time and in no time, in all events, situations and circumstances. This request extends from this day forward throughout my entire lifetime. I ask that all those who are aligned with the Divine Plan of God for my being, and all those who are aligned with the Divine Will of God for me, present themselves in help and assistance to me, in the name of God, by the power of God, Source of all Sources, through the blessing of the Holy Spirit, the feminine principle, the eternal Mother.

I bless and gratefully acknowledge that I have received in this now moment assistance and guidance from the highest source of Love and Light, and that this help and healing will stretch from Eternity to Eternity.

And so it is. It is done. Amen. I am your mother Quan Yin.

Introduction to Melchizedek

Melchizedek is our universal logos or the Word for our universe. *"In the beginning was the Word and the Word was with God and the Word was God." (John 1:1)* Melchizedek is a great cosmic being whose might, power, intensity and greatness we cannot imagine with our limited minds. As New Age advocates we can simply regard him as an Ascended Master. However, to understand his importance, I would simply state the levels and hierarchies which are under his command. Within our realms of Mastery on Earth, there are the Ascended Masters and our World Teacher. At the level of our planet we work with our planetary logos, Sanat Kumara, and the other Kumaras who work with him. Within our solar system we work with the solar logos, Lord Helios and Lady Vesta. At the galactic level we work with, or rather work is done on behalf of the entire galaxy by the galactic Logos, Lord Melchior and Lady Melchai. Finally at the universal level, Lord Melchizedek and Lady Malak hold the hierarch or Word for our universe.

Now, if you can imagine that our planetary logos has worked for millions of years to attain his position as the planetary logos, you may have a glimpse of what our universal logos had to do to be in that position. If you can comprehend that there are billions of star systems in one galaxy alone and that billions of galaxies make up a universe, then the scope becomes completely mind-boggling. The perception of such greatness is practically impossible to grasp since we do not yet even have a full understanding of the power and might that our Brothers and Sisters of the Ascended realms are capable of mustering. I therefore suggest for the sake of our limited minds and perceptions that we think of Melchizedek as a mighty, powerful, loving Ascended Master of Light, who has been around for a very long time. Let us simply accept that he is capable of guiding us to the Light throughout this lifetime and beyond. (I have given an account of one of Melchizedek's Earthly incarnations as detailed in the book of *1 Enoch* in Part IV, Introduction to Metatron and Enlightenment.)

The *Encyclopedia of Angels* says of him *"Melchizedek, Melkisedek, Melch-zadok, a king and priest in the Old Testament who in angle lore is associated with angels. Melchizedek means, "The God Zedek is my king." And he is described in the New Testament as the "King of righteousness: and the "King of peace."* (p. 237). In the book of

Genesis (14:18-20), Melchizedek is called the *"King of Salem, the priest of El-Elyon."* Abraham tithes the king and Psalm 110:4 says, *"You are a priest forever after the order of Melchizedek."* Forever takes on a new meaning when seen from the perspective of the hierarchies of time and levels of existence between us and our universal logos, Melchizedek.

Sanat Kumara, in a reading to a favorite disciple, said, *"It has taken us 125 million years to plan the project for the present evolution of the masses of Earthly souls to reach first level of initiation on the ladder of spiritual evolution."* Imagine how many billions of years it would have taken ascending the dimensions in order to reach the universal level. Suffice it to say that we have a great being who has enormous patience and compassion to bestow upon us. If we can imagine the hierarchy of the Ascended Masters as our older sisters and brothers, then Melchizedek would hold the position of a dearly beloved great grandparent who loves and cherishes us and whom we would hold in great reverence, respect and love in return.

Melchizedek on the Nature of Darkness

Commentary: In this section, Melchizedek — who is our universal logos — explains the nature of darkness. In the world of duality we automatically divide everything to opposite poles of good and bad, light and dark. We do not appreciate the truth that all is part of the oneness, and to return to oneness we must accept and love all of God's creation.

Loving all does not mean inviting it into our lives or making it part of everyday living. We can send Light and love to all of creation and yet be selective in what we wish to have in our lives and who we serve. All the flowers in God's creation are beautiful, but we do not have to plant them all in our backyard or pick them for display in our homes. We can send them love and appreciation and value each for their unique contribution.

Where the Light does not shine, there is darkness. In the absence of Light, the dark may turn into acts of evil. Acts of evil stem from the desire to create disharmony and imbalance in the fabric of Godliness. Light's mission is to establish balance in all bodies of matter, bringing peace and harmony. In this way, matter may know Godliness, its divine origin. We must remain vigilant to keep our Light shining brightly and to maintain our state of balance. Then the chaos caused by disharmony will have no room to grow or to penetrate into our lives.

MELCHIZEDEK, CHANNELED SEPTEMBER 12, 2004

Beloveds, I am your brother, Melchizedek.

Remember, dark is not evil. Dark is the entity of everything that has taken a body of matter. Light is the spark of divinity that is blown into that entity of matter. **Anything that has mass holds darkness. And by the same token, it holds the spark of Light. It is our job (the beings of Light) to illuminate the dark with the Light.** It is the job of the Dark Lords to test us to see if we can maintain the Light before we are allowed to completely surrender to that Light and become one with it. Evil is the product of mass on its journey into darkness, forgetting its unity and Light and moving into the energy of fear. All the negative emotions are fear-based.

There is a great misunderstanding in your world regarding light and dark, good and bad. Dark is not necessarily evil. However, the chance of dark turning into evil is greater than Light turning into evil. The dark lords are equally worthy of praise for the work that they do. Their work is also an act of service. I suggest that you should honor the presence of dark because it is a celebration of Light. How else would you be able to understand Light in a world of duality unless you had an understanding of darkness? How else would you understand joy unless you had an experience of pain? How else would you know the expression of happiness unless you have known the expression of sorrow? How else would you find Light within yourself unless you have searched for, found the dark and released it from your being? Always, put the Light before you, above you, behind you, below you, within you, around you, always. But remain respectful that the purpose of dark is to teach you and to allow you to embody the Light.

Remember you are a universe. You are a microcosm which reflects the macrocosm. Within your own limited bodies and beings, you are a universe. As above, so below. As within, so without.

May the Light always shine upon your path. Come to replenish yourself with the energies of the universal sun, the Melchizedek Principle. Breathe deeply now as you come into the Presence of the Pure White Light to visit Lord Melchizedek and Lady Malak (his female counterpart). Take a deep breath, and pause here. Say a prayer, express a desire or wish and wait for a while for a sign, a word, a profusion of light or a symbol. Ask for a boon (gift). Bathe in the Pure White Light. Be touched. Expand. Receive.

Pray for Light. Pray for illumination. Pray for your personal intent. Pause, breathe and meditate. When you feel complete, you may begin to return.

Let us bless our good fortune in this togetherness. We will descend from the universal level through the galactic level to the solar level. We are recalibrating in the presence of Lord Helios and Lady Vesta, the deities of our sun. (They are the father and mother energies for all the planets and the consciousness of this entire solar system.) Receive a blessing from the presence of Lord Helios and Lady Vesta. Pause and take a deep breath as you stage your intention and ask for a sign.

I bring you back from the solar system, planet by planet, back into the heartcore of Mother Earth and into your own body. Settling yourself back in the body, feel your own energy from the top of your head to the bottom of your feet. Hold yourself in the state of peace and harmony, and repeat this exercise regularly to maintain your peace.

In celebration of Light and in honor of the oneness of all, I am your brother, Melchizedek. So it is.

Part Two ~ Healing

Introduction to Healing and Mother Mary

As human beings, we are made of a collective consciousness consisting of our bodies, our senses and emotions, our minds, our soul and spirit. Inside the physical body we are encapsulated in matter. Matter is condensed and solidified energy. The more solid the matter becomes the more darkness and dross it will attract. That darkness creates pain. Pain causes distortion and brings us, our bodies, minds, emotions, soul and spirit to a halt, delaying our progress and retarding our happiness.

THE PROBLEM

Accumulation of pain causes depression and that leads to further darkness. It dulls the mind and numbs the senses. To free ourselves from all this, we resort to healing. Healing must be applied in all levels of our body and beingness because deep within our core our hearts, minds, emotions, soul and spirit are affected. Ancient Chinese medicine states that the root cause of all physical ailments is in the mind and the emotions. Quantum physics tells us this whole universe is a byproduct of our mind, and sages of the East tell us that this entire manifest creation is an illusion of the mind. The quantum physicists are now able to demonstrate that one atom of matter can simultaneously exist and operate in more than one place. (See documentary movie "What the Bleep Do We Know?") This being the case, we should be able to heal our bodies and emotions through our minds. All those atoms of matter and substance which can occupy more than one space at each given time can come to our rescue and recreate a world free from pain and suffering.

An Australian boy was hit by a car while walking on the street. His leg was amputated from mid-thigh. The surgery went well and he was sent home. After a few months, his parents noticed tissue growing where his amputated leg used to be. In a frenzy, they took the boy back to the hospital. The surgeons and their medical team anxiously examined the boy to see what anomaly had caused the little boy to start growing his leg again. In the middle of the chaos, the little boy plucked up enough courage to ask what was wrong. He was told that he was growing back his leg. Now he was really puzzled. He said to them, "I have seen my pet lizards and the geckos which I play with grow their legs after they lose them in accidents. I was doing the same. If they can do it, why shouldn't I?"

The grown-ups paused, aghast for a moment, only to compose themselves and inform the little boy in their great wisdom, "Yes, but human beings do not grow legs!" After those wise words the growth of the leg stopped. The limitation of the grown-ups' mindset had done its damage. It caused the little boy's mind to believe the grown ups instead of the truth he had experienced for himself. Until then his mind was set to grow a new leg and he was proving it possible. Indeed, if lizards and geckos can grow limbs, why can't we? After all, are we not the more intelligent species? Scientific experiments have proven that the larger the size of the brain, the greater the capacity of the intellect, leading to higher intelligence and greater achievements of the species. With much greater brain capacity, why can we not heal ourselves from ailments, grow limbs, cleanse our internal organs, tissues and cells, prevent deterioration and heal ourselves to enjoy longer, happier lives?

Our ancestors who sat in the ark and fled from the flood lived to be hundreds of years old. The scriptures tell us that Noah lived to be 900. In fact, for many generations before and after Noah, scriptures show life spans of 300 to 900 years. Why is it then, that we do not live long lives? Our genetic strands remain the same, and no deterioration or anomalies have been discovered in our brain capacities or in our genetic heritage since the time of Noah. On the contrary, the conditions of our lives have improved. The mechanized world is making life so much easier to live. Why then are we not striving to live longer lives? Why does the average lifespan of people of the first world not surpass much farther beyond eighty years and those of the developing and underdeveloped world even shorter? And why are there so many rampant diseases?

Could it be the state of our minds and our rampant uncontrollable emotions? This coupled with an overpopulated and polluted planet who is incapable of clearing and cleansing herself as fast as we manage to pollute and destroy her? Could it be that the quotient of light has dwindled since the time of Noah and through the lineage of our ancestors? Could it be that our communion with nature and our belief in goodness and healing has been shaken down? If these were indeed the answers then, could we make a turn-around by adopting the ways of our ancestors? By returning to love and communion with nature, working with the Light and bringing healing love to each other, can we experience a higher quality of life and live longer?

I believe we can, and the Masters of Light tell us that we can. In fact, the Masters are extremely hopeful for us. In spite of the world disasters — natural and man-made events — the Masters have already begun singing the praises of our entry into the Seventh Golden Age. This is the Golden Age of Wisdom and Truth whose emblem is an eagle. The Mayan prophecies call it the Age of "Itza", or knowledge. This is why healing is an important and integral part of this new Golden Age. To begin on this path we will need to rebuild our world and our bodies through healing ourselves and our planet. We must begin with curative as well as preventative measures to heal ourselves and our planet simultaneously. If we only focus on curing ourselves, we will then continue to play catch up with ourselves and our world. Simply curing does not stop us from over-polluting and overpopulating, over-emotionalizing and mentally over-emphasizing our bodies and our world. It will also help to take preventative measures reducing the over-build-up of technology and reestablishing our connection with Mother Nature and all natural things.

The experts in social behavior say of the echo-boomers (the generations of souls born since the 1970's) that they have no concept of the real world outside, nor do they have any ideas about connection or communication with nature. Their parents who are from generations of baby boomers have spoiled them and have treated them as though they were made of fragile porcelain. This is because the baby boomers themselves are the children of war-stricken parents who have instilled values and appreciation for life upon their baby boomer children. The baby boomers have in turn gone to what seems to be the extreme. Therefore, their children have been affected by the unreal world of computer games and information technology. The echo-boomers expect instant gratification and constant praise when they perform the simplest of tasks. They require instant feedback without which they cannot function or go to the next task.

Some of these souls are young adults and have entered into the real world of business trade and politics. According to specialists in the world of social behavior, they have very little concept of reality and ability to interact with each other. We must find a cure for this anomalous situation and prevent the future generations of our children from following suit. Our young adults and the children entering into the world need to learn to cope with real world situations, not the assimilated systems whose function and outcome we have customized for them through computers. Children and young adults are striving to find new ways to cope with real life situations themselves. I have many inquiries from them regarding the healing and meditation classes. In my experience once they find the way, they take to it as fish to water and quickly gain the means to cope.

Obviously, curative measures alone will not be the only solutions. Prevention must accompany every curative situation. Now we have to plan to heal our seas and oceans from pollution, our air from gaseous fumes and the green house effect in the ozone layer, our children from unreal simulated life games, our bodies from over-processed foods, our minds from over-stress and our emotions from over-exaggerated and rampant feelings.

For all of the above, there are healing measures which can give us maps to the unknown and shortcuts to greater health and wholeness in all aspects of our lives and bodies.

These healings also benefit the life force of the body and the future of Mother Earth, upon which our children and our grandchildren shall be born and will thrive.

There is always a first step in every process of healing. The first step may not itself be our major "Aha" moment, but it will be a means to that end. The first step is to understand and accept that in order to heal our bodies we must be willing to look at ourselves as a conglomerate of beings. **Our consciousness has as great a need to be healed as our bodies do, and the two work together.** Once we can accept that, then we can move into the healing process. The substance of our consciousness is made of finer matter or energy. In fact, everything in this physically manifest universe of matter is made of energy. Matter is condensed energy. If we accept this scientifically proven premise, then we should not have any difficulty accepting that in order to heal our world of matter — which is made of condensed energy — we need to use energy healing. If energy is the building block of our substance and our existence, then it stands to reason that energy healing can be the means to relieve the ailments of our energy bodies of matter.

The greatest healing energy is light. The greatest and the purest of light which we can call to ourselves can come to us through our brothers and sisters of the Ascended realms. They work with light and energies of the highest potency. They are awaiting our call to bring the healing lights to relieve us from our ailments and to offer us not just cures but prevention.

In this section we will address cures through the healing light and touch of the Masters. I have chosen Mother Mary and Archangel Raphael as our two illuminating guides. Archangel Raphael's name means "God has healed." An angel of God's presence, Raphael is the healer of not only humanity but also angels and planets.

Mother Mary works closely with Archangel Raphael. In the *Encyclopedia of Angels* it is stated: *"Ex-canonical works such as the book of John the evangelist refer to Mary as being an angel herself. Apochryphal New Testament says that she is the angel sent by God to receive the Lord."* (p. 236). Some New Age literature states that Mother Mary and Raphael are twin rays (twin flames) and are from the same healing ray and lineage of light (Luke, p. 291). Mother Mary has been extremely active in offering healing to humanity in the past 2000 years. Her apparitions all across the world have caused mass healings. Healing waters have appeared at her apparition sites. People have had miraculous healing in Lourdes France, Fatima Portugal, Barcelona Spain, Ezmir Turkey, Medjegoria Bosnia, Guadalupe Mexico, LaSalette France, Knock Ireland and Beauring Banneaux in Belgium (Guiley, p. 232).

There is a small chapel in Ezmir, Turkey where some believe that Mother Mary spent the last three years of her life. This is a small house which was later turned into a chapel on top of a hill with rolling greens and a winding brook in the outskirts of Ezmir. My trip to Ezmir was one of those miraculous events orchestrated by the Masters.

Three groups of us had come together in the year 2000 to perform ceremonies for bringing light to the new millennium. Each group had been instructed by Metatron to go to a specific part of the world anchoring light. We were all to meet at our final destination in Istanbul, Turkey. My group was the last to arrive amid delays in catching connecting flights. We were fraught with all manner of travel problems as well as deep exhaustion and sickness from various foods and the change of climate. We were coming from India. Our sacred pilgrimage had taken us a very long time. When we arrived in Istanbul, Turkey the other two groups had found out that Mother Mary's site in Ezmir was a short plane ride away. The only problem was that the plane flew there only once a week. The next flight was early the following morning. That meant we would only have a brief rest of a few hours before we had to be airborne again. The decision was left to members of my group because we were the most tired and the latest arrivals. We all agreed to go ahead. Very early the next morning we boarded the airport bus outside of our hotel for the destination of Ezmir, Turkey. As we were waiting for all the group members to embark, my friend Lucille's son Christopher, who had become a regular participant in our travels and ceremonies, planted a kiss on my cheek and said, "Happy Mother's Day, Nas!" Tears came to my eyes when I realized that Mother Mary had invited us to her last home on Mother's Day.

While we were in that small chapel, I could feel the subtle energy which is so typical of Mother Mary's presence. I thanked her for her love and told her that with this gift she has given me, the confirmation that our work had been successful and that she was pleased with our efforts. I also told her that besides the site of Lady of Guadalupe in

Mexico and now here in Ezmir, I had not been invited to any other of her apparition sites. I asked that she would please consider calling me to those places. I felt left out when I had traveled around the entire globe three times in less than two years and had not been to any of Mother Mary's numerous apparition sites. This I said and went about my way enjoying the energies and ceremonies. Within one year from that day I had visited six of her apparition sites. Such is the love of a true compassionate Mother.

Mother Mary's greatest gift to us is her healing through her prayers. She prays as she heals and she heals through her loving prayers. She always beckons us to heal through prayer, forgiveness and love.

Mother Mary is an Ascended Master who serves the light and helps humankind through her loving compassionate guidance, healing and prayers. She is known as the Queen of Peace, Queen of Heaven, and she is an aspect of Divine Mother. *The Encyclopedia of Angels* by Rosemary Ellen Guiley recounts titles attributed to Mary: *"Queen of Angels," "Our Lady of the Angels," "Blessed Virgin," "Virgin Mary," and "Our Lady"* (p. 235).

She also says this regarding Mary's immaculate conception: *"Because Mary was destined to be the Mother of Christ, God infused her soul with grace at the moment of her conception in the womb of her mother, St. Ann. Her immaculate conception is announced by the Archangel Gabriel (Luke 1:26-28). Gabriel tells her that the Holy Spirit will come upon her in order that she may conceive her son. The immaculate conception was rejected by St.*

Thomas Aquinas in the 13th century. Many modern theologians consider the immaculate conception to be symbolic and not literal" (p. 235).

The focus of this book and my reference point to Mother Mary is in her capacity as an Ascended Master, a spiritual guide and healer of all humankind and as a Goddess, feminine principle, or a Divine Mother. According to New Age understanding, Mary became an Ascended Master at the end of her lifetime as the mother of Jesus. By the end of that lifetime she had provided great service and healing light to humankind.

In her lifetimes before that of Mary, mother of Jesus, she had been trained to attain levels of Mastery which prepared her for the lifetime as the mother to the Messiah. Jesus from our reference point is the Christed one, the one who realized the Christed Self within himself. He came to bring the energies of divine love to Earth and to the hearts of humankind. It is a belief in New Age literature that both Mary and her husband Joseph (St. Germain in a later lifetime) were great Masters, healers and teachers in their own right and were fully aware of the perfect design and the divine plan for themselves, for their child and for Earth. They came to fulfill this plan and pave the path for their son, Master Jesus. Up to that point the image of the God of the Old Testament was one of wrath, anger and vengeance. The image of God that Jesus portrayed was one of love, tolerance and acceptance. Furthermore, unconditional love and acceptance were qualities promoted by Jesus and exemplified in his own life.

In his living, he showed us the frailties of body and his enduring pains, fears and struggles. In his dying, he showed us how to embrace all those negative qualities through the worst of circumstances. In his resurrection, he showed us the power to overcome those frailties, pains, fears and struggles and how to master them. Jesus is an Ascended Master; a very powerful and extremely compassionate older brother who has been tried and tested by the worst of circumstances in physical embodiment on Earth. He not only hears us and feels our pain, he knows it. He knows the experience of the worst kind of pains — physical, emotional, mental and spiritual — and he has the compassion to come to our rescue.

The same applies to his mother, Mary, who was his teacher and a teacher to the Essene people of her time. She was a healer and a seer, a visionary who knew about the cross she had to bear on behalf of humanity through her son. As any parent would probably agree, worse than dying is seeing your child die before your eyes. Mother Mary is such a Master. She mastered the physical body and its emotions through her strict observance of the Essene ways of truth. She too knows about the pain of being in physicality.

When we call to her for healing, help, guidance and nurturance, she gives wholeheartedly. She continues to serve all in pursuit of truth, light and goodness, and she is evermore powerful and determined, gentle and compassionate toward us all whom she calls her children. She is evermore giving and present to help, to guide and to pray with us and for us and to intercede on our behalfalf.

Dr. Edmond Bordeaux Szekely is a scholar and researcher of ancient manuscripts found in the secret archives of Vatican information, which he translated and collected in book form called *The Essene Gospel of Peace*. Book one of this series was published in 1928. Books two, three and four followed. Book four, *The Teachings of the Elect*, was published two years after his death in 1979, according to instructions he left behind and through the efforts of his wife and successor, Norma Nilsson Bordeaux Szekely.

In *Book One* of the *Essene Gospel of Peace*, Master Jesus is quoted to have praised and spoken of the Kingdom of our Earthly Mother with equal respect as that of the Heavenly Father:

"For your Heavenly Father is love, for your Earthly Mother is love, for the Son of Man is love. It is by love, that the Heavenly Father and the Earthly Mother and the Son of Man become one. For the spirit of the Son of Man was created from the spirit of the Heavenly Father, and his body from the body of the Earthly Mother. Become, therefore, perfect as the spirit of your Heavenly Father and the body of your Earthly Mother are perfect. And so love your Heavenly Father, as he loves your spirit. And so love your Earthly Mother, as she loves your body" (p. 19).

Then Master Jesus gives his disciples the prayer to the Heavenly Father followed by the prayer to the Early Mother:

"Therefore, pray to your Heavenly Father: Our Father which art in Heaven, hallowed be Thy name. Thy kingdom come. Thy will be done on Earth as it is in Heaven. Give us this day our daily bread. And forgive us our debts, as we forgive our debtors. And lead us not into temptation, but deliver us from evil. For Thine

*is the kingdom, the power and the glory, forever. Amen.
And after this manner pray to your Earthly Mother:
Our Mother which art upon Earth, hallowed be Thy
name. Thy kingdom come, and Thy will be done in us,
as it is in Thee. As Thou send every day Thy angels,
send them to us also. Forgive us our sins, as we atone
all our sins against Thee. And lead us not into sickness, but deliver us from all evil. For Thine is the Earth,
the body and the health. Amen." (p. 47).*

Over the course of time, only the Our Father portion of
this prayer was practiced and the Our Mother portion was
forgotten. The Essene people respected and honored the
motherly aspect embodied by Earth herself equally with the
fatherly aspect as the heavenly spirit that moves through
the body. This is in keeping with other traditions and
cultures of Earth, especially that of the Native American
and Aboriginal people of Australia and New Zealand where
Father Sky and Mother Earth are blessed and honored
equally and remembered at the beginning and ending of all
ceremonies and rituals. You may choose to add the Our
Mother portion to your Prayer of the Rosary or whenever
you feel drawn to recite the Our Father prayer.

In the pages that follow, you will read Mother Mary's
request to recite the Prayer of the Rosary. We have heeded
her request and printed the prayer in this section. This is a
powerful tool to connect to the energies of divine grace
which are bestowed upon Mary for her service to humankind. In turn, she brings the blessing to us as we unite with
her in the repetition of Our Father and Hail Mary prayer.

She has said in many readings to people of all faiths that the prayer is an effective tool for changing our world and bringing peace to the hearts of humankind.

The energy that transpires from the repetition is not bound by the limitations of the words and surpasses religion, faith and belief systems. In the higher realms, these prayers are recited in sound syllables containing energy forms which are not limited to the meaning of the words. Words truly cannot carry the extent of the potency of the essence of these prayers, and yet words are our mode of communication in this three-dimensional realm of reality. The energy is therefore contained in the words. When we go beyond the limitation of the words and our personal interface issues, we will be touched by the energies in an amazingly effective and potent way. The least of the experiences that you can expect is the peace and serenity that fills the air and the knowing that through this connection, Mother Mary is watching, hearing and applying the vibration of love contained within the prayer.

My first introduction to the Prayer of the Rosary was in the early days after my arrival in the United States of America. After attending mass in a Catholic church, I was deep in meditation when someone tapped me on the shoulder and asked if I would like to join the Prayer of the Rosary. Hearing the word "prayer," I said yes before I knew what it was. The person handed me a plastic rosary and moved on. I noticed that a small group of people, each holding their prayer beads, were sitting in pews close to each other. I watched them and followed the sound of their voices. One person led the beginning of a sentence and everyone joined to finish each line. Since I did not have the words, I closed my eyes and listened to the sounds of their voices. The prayer was being recited too fast for me to decipher every word. I became still as the energy of the prayer began to ebb and flow its way into my heart. It filled my heart and brought great peace and serenity. I became still.

After the prayers, I asked where I could find the words to the prayer, and I was directed to the brochure shelf at the entrance. It was fortunate that I had experienced the energy of the prayer before I read the words, because I found myself getting stuck in some of the terms. For example, in reciting the Hail Mary portion, I had difficulty calling myself a sinner and asking Mother Mary to pray for me, "the sinner." It felt as though I was putting the burden of responsibility on her to cleanse me of my sins, as if I had no part nor any responsibility for my actions. Born in Muslim faith, my discovery of the Christian church came after my opening to the spiritual light and after I had studied and exercised Hindu and Buddhist beliefs, as well as Islam. Mother Mary herself was a familiar and favorite character, because as a child I would listen to stories of her in the Quran (Koran), read and retold to us by our nanny. Mother Mary, known as Mariam, (or Maryam) has her own chapter (chapter or sura 19) by that name in the Quran.

I continued to attend the Prayer of the Rosary every morning in the church and cringed every time we came to the last line. But I persisted and became immersed in an energy of peace that brought immeasurable comfort. One day after the prayer ended I sat alone in the church, very quiet and peaceful but very sad and lonely. I was looking at the beautiful statue of Mother Mary. I closed my eyes and asked her to give me solace during these hard times. Suddenly I heard the loving and gentle voice which said to me,

"My beloved child of light, I am your Mother Mary." She proceeded to tell me that the Prayer of the Rosary would help me out of the hardship and that I must seriously consider reciting the entire prayer for each of the three mysteries ten times each day. That is a total of over 1500 Hail Marys and more than 150 Our Fathers along with other short prayers to complete the entire prayer in the correct manner. She told me that if I continued to do this daily for three months my life would completely change, and that phase of pain and sorrow would come to an end.

I seriously began this amazing journey. At first, the hours would go by and although I had not finished the full course of the prayer, the bliss that I felt was phenomenal! Gradually, I developed a system where in the course of three and a half hours, I could complete the task. The result was a state of total peace throughout the day and a great sleep during the night. I fell asleep at night with my rosary in hand, reciting the prayer to get ahead on the next day's round or to catch up with what I had missed during the day. This resulted in lucid dreams of angels and light-beings. When I would awaken, my mind automatically resumed the prayers, and I could hear them in my head all the time.

After three months, my external life did change very dramatically. But more importantly, my inner world and my outlook to the world had changed. I no longer felt lonely and helpless, nor did I fear this unknown world of extremes that I had entered. My inner peace and calm and my knowingness that I was loved and protected by the angels and the prayers of Mother Mary were the greatest gifts and most valuable lessons during that very difficult period of my life.

In many readings, Mother Mary requests of my clients and students to recite the Prayer of the Rosary for their personal needs and for world peace. She maintains her position that no matter which faith, religion or belief system we come from, the Prayer of the Rosary will benefit us and the world. It magnifies her ability to intercede on our behalf because of the accumulated energy of all the rosary prayers ever recited before.

Once during my travels, Mother Mary appeared at the beginning of a life reading and specifically asked a woman to say the Prayer of the Rosary for the upcoming events in her life and for world peace. The woman told me after her reading that she was tempted to get up and leave right after that information because had I been genuinely channeling a Master, they would know that she was born to the Jewish faith and practiced her faith with great zest and fervor. Fortunately, curiosity got the best of her. She stayed on to hear Mother Mary give her important information relevant to her life and helpful for her future, as well as great healing of the traumas of the past.

One sign that helped remove her anger and doubt was when Mother Mary reminded her of a time when, against all odds, she had helped a family move through the mourning phase of the loss of a loved one. Her assistance in this situation was very well appreciated in the higher realms. After the event, Mother Mary had appeared to her in a dream. With her hands in prayer pose, Mother Mary had bowed to her in thanksgiving. The woman had not told this dream to anyone. She could not figure out why Mother Mary would appear to her in her dream since she was not of Christian faith. And why would Mother Mary bow to her in thanksgiving? She did not connect the dream to the help she had given to the mourning family. When Mother Mary related the two incidents together in the life reading, the client burst out crying in love and gratitude. After the session, she recounted both her doubts and gratitude.

In a reading given by Master Hilarion in May of 2005, Mother Mary requested this, through Hilarion: "Mother Mary would like to ask that you would say the Prayer of the Rosary as many times as you can in the course of each day and night. She is asking that you would take a rosary with you to bed. She says that when you fall asleep following the Prayer of the Rosary or even mid-sentence while saying it, that your soul will be given the chance to move to higher realms of consciousness and that she will be granted permission to take your soul to the retreats where wisdom and understanding are dispersed by the Masters. She says the Prayer of the Rosary is a lot more than the words. It is the energy. In those higher realms there are sounds and syllables that translate to the Prayer of the Rosary in your realm but are very highly potent in encapsulating the energies of healing and raising the consciousness of the soul. Mother Mary says, 'To accelerate the pace of your soul growth, to raise the vibration of your soul and to connect your soul with the personality say the Prayer of the Rosary.'"

Prayer of the Rosary

Three versions of the Prayer of the Rosary are included here: traditional Christian, the original Essene version and the New Age version. Whichever one resonates with you, you are encouraged to follow Mother Mary's request to "Pray. Pray. Pray."

To recite one round of the Prayer of the Rosary you need to say one Our Father followed by ten Hail Marys, and then repeat this sequence five times. This is the simplified version which is a good start. Before you start, sit in meditation, still your mind and say, "*I offer this prayer for peace on Earth and for my personal intentions (state your intentions). I unite myself in prayer with Mother Mary and ask her help and the intercessions of all the Masters of Light to magnify these prayers in the name of the I AM THAT I AM.*" Then begin by one Our Father, ten Hail Marys and one Glory Be. Do this five times, and you will have completed one round of the Prayer of the Rosary.

OUR FATHER (TRADITIONAL CHRISTIAN)

Our Father who art in Heaven, hallowed by Thy name. Thy Kingdom come, Thy will be done on Earth as it is in Heaven. Give us this day our daily bread and forgive us our trespasses, as we forgive those who trespass against us. Lead us not into temptation and deliver us from evil. For Thine is the kingdom and the power and glory, now and forever, Amen.

HAIL MARY (TRADITIONAL CHRISTIAN)

Hail Mary, full of grace, the Lord is with Thee. Blessed are Thou among women and blessed is the fruit of Thy womb, Jesus. Holy Mary, mother of God, pray for us sinners now and at the hour of our death. Amen.

GLORY BE (TRADITIONAL CHRISTIAN)

Glory be to the Father and the Son and the Holy Spirit. As it was in the beginning, is now and ever shall be. Amen.

If you feel drawn, you may do as many repetitions as you can. To obtain a rosary and the long version of the prayers, you can stop at a religious store or a Catholic church. Many people use their fingers to count the numbers as they say the prayer, and it works just as well.

Below is the Essene version of the prayer of Our Father and Our Mother as stated in the teachings of Master Jesus and translated by Edmond Bordeaux Szekely in *The Essene Gospel of Peace*. The Our Father portion of the prayer is very similar to the traditional Christian prayer. However, as you see, the Our Mother portion is completely missing from the traditional Christian prayer. It is an important and integral piece for these reasons:

1. It restores the balance of feminine and masculine by acknowledging the Mother aspect and holding it in respect and reverence alongside the Father aspect.

2. It restores balance to Mother Earth and invokes the Angels of Earthly Mother to bless us and Earth together.

3. It reconnects us (the human beings) with our Mother (the Earth) and brings healing to Earth and to us. It can serve as a reminder that as our Mother, we must hold her in respect and reverence and treat her as we ideally would treat our human mothers.

4. It will enable us to enter into the flow of abundance and assistance which comes from Earth to us. After all, let us be reminded that all the resources which bring us comfort, luxury, peace and harmony are from Earth.

OUR FATHER (ESSENE)
Our Father which art in Heaven, hallowed be Thy name. Thy kingdom come. Thy will be done on Earth as it is in Heaven. Give us this day our daily bread. And forgive us

our debts, as we forgive our debtors. And lead us not into temptation, but deliver us from evil. For Thine is the kingdom, the power and the glory, forever. Amen.

OUR MOTHER (ESSENE)

Our Mother which art upon Earth, hallowed be Thy name. Thy kingdom come, and Thy will be done in us, as it is in Thee. As Thou send every day Thy angels, send them to us also. Forgive us our sins, as we atone all our sins against Thee. And lead us not into sickness, but deliver us from all evil. For Thine is the Earth, the body and the health. Amen.

ROSARY OF THE NEW AGE

Hail Mother, full of grace, the Lord is with Thee. Blessed art Thou amongst women and blessed is the fruit of Thy womb I AM. Hold for us now the immaculate concept of our true God Reality from this moment unto our eternal ascension in the light of the I AM THAT I AM. (For the full text, go to www.1spirit.com Sept 04, 2005 Newsletter. For further info on this event, go to www.worldpuja.org.)

Cocoon of Protection for Healers

Commentary: This discourse was given to someone who had received training in healing and recently started her own healing practice. Working on releasing energies from the bodies and emotions of her clients, she had grown weary, fatigued, depressed and experienced a constant low energy state. Her mind was dull and foggy. To function she needed to take naps during the day and to go to bed early at night. Mother Mary gave her the cocoon of protection healing meditation. She says the purpose of this meditation is to help you open up to receive and to encapsulate your own body and energy in the pure light of the I AM, so that you are replenished when you give healing to others. If you do this practice for 22 days without a break, it becomes part of your own being and it will never leave you. After that, all you need to do is occasionally call upon it, to enhance it and to remind yourself that you have protection.

It is important to realize that this is given not just for professional healers, but for all of us. We heal and teach one another through our relationships during difficult times and good times alike. Sometimes in the sharing of this richness of life we can become drained. It is at those times when we call upon Mother Mary and the Prayer of the Rosary to replenish us.

MOTHER MARY, CHANNELED AUGUST 26, 2004

My children of Light, I am your Mother Mary.

In the course of this healing, I shall call upon the levels and dimensions of higher light to bring you assistance and protection. From now on, whether you are teaching or healing someone in person or from a distance, you will feel yourself refreshed and replenished after the session. This I can do for you when you ask my intercession to bring healing to you and to energize you. **The process can be enhanced when you say the Prayer of the Rosary.** For this reason I ask you to give a lot of importance to the Prayer of the Rosary and to never be without it. Even if one day you miss the chance to say your prayer, make sure that the next day you pick it up and you say it more intently. The emphasis is not so much on the number of times that you say it but on your continuous connection with me and with the Prayer of the Rosary.

Two purposes are served from working with the Prayer of the Rosary: 1) to encapsulate your own energy in the light of this prayer and to raise your vibration to a higher level, and 2) to unite your energies and prayers with the energies of all the Prayers of the Rosary that have ever been said on behalf of humankind. These include those that my legions and I (Mother Mary) say before the Throne of Grace. Many Prayers of the Rosary are constantly performed, and many prayer vigils are constantly held at all times.

When you say the Prayer of the Rosary, I take that prayer and unite it with all the prayers that have ever been said, are now being said and shall ever be said again. Then the potency and the intensity of the energy is magnified. The pool of energy of all the Prayers of the Rosary is constantly increased and is available to each of you who say the prayers. Imagine if you say one Prayer of the Rosary, and not just your voice but the voices of multitudes are added to yours. And with that force I can accelerate the outcome and bring results to you. With the accumulated power and force of the multitudes and my intercessions, your intention can bear fruit.

I am here with you to teach you to protect yourself. To this end, I will invoke Archangel Michael to bring you the shield of mercy. The shield helps to raise your own light energy. As you give this light to others, you must constantly replenish yourself. The purpose of Archangel Michael's shield of mercy is to protect your light, the light which you can raise and give to your patients and clients. The light is raised and maintained within you. Your body can use as much as it needs in any given moment. The shield will protect the light from leaking. By encapsulating the light inside of your own body, it helps boost your energy to reach the higher realms where you can see, visualize and hear guidance.

The benefits are threefold: 1) to fill you with light energy for personal use. This will prevent you from depleting yourself 2) to protect you from draining your energy out of your body or absorbing lower vibrational energies 3) to enable you to give a higher calibration of the energy to your clients and your patients.

To administer this process, I ask Archangel Michael to place the shield of mercy around you. Archangel Michael will call upon his legions to perform this task. Meanwhile, I send you the energies of the golden pink flame of Divine Love to energize you and to boost your body and beingness. At the same time, I will be calling upon the magnification of the Prayer of the Rosary. This process will take a few minutes.

Meanwhile, I want you to say the Prayer of the Rosary, starting with one Our Father and then ten Hail Marys. Consciously go into the energy of the prayer to receive and absorb the light. It is beneficial to spend ten minutes each day to repeat this process. Set aside time daily for meditation and to say the Prayer of the Rosary. When you learn the prayer by heart — without the need to read the instructions — you will feel the energies even more. Do I have your permission to administer this healing energy upon you? If you would like to receive from Mother Mary, say, *"Yes."*

Take a deep breath. I call upon the presence of Archangel Michael and the legions of Michael to form a circle of light around the body of (*say your name*). I call the presence of all your loved ones and family members to receive from this shield of Light and shield of mercy as well. They will each receive their own shield of protection. We call upon their Higher Selves of all to be present. Now call the names of your family members and loved ones that you wish to receive this shield. (For example, "*I call upon my son, James and his Higher Self to receive the shield of mercy.*")

The legions of Michael form circles around each individual's bodies, with their swords of mercy held above their heads. The sword is drawn out of its sheath, and it emits an electric blue light. (The vibration of electric blue is much like the sword that Luke Skywalker held in the Star Wars movies.) The tips of the swords held by the multitudes of the legions touch, a dome of blue light is created over the head of each individual (*say everyone's name*). The blue light forms a pillar of light that surrounds the bodies of everyone receiving it. The entire circle is filled with pure electric blue light. It is pouring down to everyone's body.

Envision that I, Mother Mary, am standing in front of you, facing you and each group member. My hands are held out. The palms of my hands are upright pointing to the palms of your hands, and my heart is facing your heart. I begin to emit the golden-pink light of Divine Love from the palms of my hands and from my heart.

A dispensation from the Throne of Grace is given to the Masters to bring new energy. It is intended for those working with the Masters. The purpose of this energy ray is to encapsulate you in the higher dimensional energy of divine love from the feminine principle. The blue light emanating from the sword of Archangel Michael is the light of

Divine Love in its power aspect. The golden pink light from my heart is Divine Love in the feminine aspect. Coming from the heart of the Source these two energies mix, and together they create a balance in your bodies. I will send you the emanation of the feminine golden pink light of Divine Love, and through the Shield of Mercy Archangel Michael and his legions send you the blue light of divine love in its masculine form. Energy flows freely from the palm of my hands and from my heart to the palm of your hands and to your heart.

I now call upon Archangel Raphael, and the legions of Raphael to stand over my presence and to create a dome of light with their swords of compassion and divine love over my head and yours. You will continue to stand under the shower of the pink light from me, and the blue light from the legions of Michael. The blue light is coming to you from above your head, emanating in the circle where you stand. The pink light is coming to you from the palms of my hand and from the circle that is created around me by Raphael, as well as from the center of my heart. Now, we call upon the magnification of the Prayer of the Rosary recited by the angelic forces of Light above my head and yours. We ask for the magnification of all the light and healing to be received by you and your loved ones.

In the name of the I AM THAT I AM, I call forth the shield of mercy to be lowered around your body from the top of the dome where the tips of the swords of mercy are touching and placed around your body. A 24-Karat liquid gold light is poured down. It reaches above your crown chakra and begins to form a cocoon around your body, like a shield of protection. Your auric field has been gold-leafed.

Around the area of your throat, your thymus gland and your chest, the golden shield is thicker (two inches) because this is the area where you deplete yourself. This is the area where lower vibrations can penetrate. When we form the thick shield around your chest, then any energies of lower vibration will be transmuted upon contact and turned into Pure White Light. In the areas where you simply need an encapsulation of your own energy, this shield is thinner. And in the areas where you need extra protection, the shield is thicker. As this gold is poured over the surface of your skin, it cocoons your body and around your aura, your energy body.

Breathe deeply now. The golden pink that your Mother Mary and Archangel Raphael are sending you is mixing with the pure electric blue light that Archangel Michael is bringing to you from the heartcore of God, the Undifferentiated Source. The divine principle of feminine and the divine principle of masculine mix and merge. The blue and pink — with the gold to seal it — unite in your energy field. The golden cocoon of light — the golden shield — will protect each one of you from this moment on from any lower vibration and from depletion.

Take a deep breath and become aware of your body and your energy. I thank Archangel Michael and his legions and Archangel Raphael and her legions. And in this instance I use the masculine aspect of Lord Michael and feminine aspect of Archangel Raphael. Raphael is the Angel of Ministration, Angel of Healing, Angel of Music, Angel of Freedom. Michael is the Angel of Mercy, Angel of Protection, Angel of Prevention from all harm. We thank them for their presence.

I hold you in my own arms. I am your Mother Mary.

Introduction to Archangel Raphael

Archangel Raphael's name means "God has healed." Raphael heals the entire Earth with her healing power. She is one of the most beloved of God's angels. Raphael has been sent to rescue humanity from all harm which befalls them on Earth, and she is the guardian of the Sun. The guide for travelers and protector of youth, Raphael is usually depicted with a musical instrument or with a staff and a cloth bag of fish. Raphael is the angel to call to administer healing in time of disasters such as earthquakes, floods and hurricanes. Raphael brought healing to Noah and helped him to build the ark and heal his people after the flood.

Raphael is one of the most frequently painted and illustrated of the angels. The poet Milton has written poems about Archangel Raphael in the company of Adam and Eve. Raphael is also known as the rescuer of all humankind from death and the healer of all ills, as well as the remover of darkness. Raphael created a golden magical ring for King Solomon, which he wore throughout his life. The significance of the ring was to assist Solomon to rule in wisdom and to protect him from untruths and injustice. With this ring, King Soloman conquered evil forces and built the Great Temple to house the Ark of the Covenant.

During my private channeling and life readings as well as in lectures and workshops, the Masters call upon Raphael to administer healing to the participants wherever necessary. These healings are given for problems which range from physical ills to emotional trauma and heartache, for mental clarity, spiritual growth and sometimes for removing trauma from other lifetimes which are impacting this lifetime. Masters call upon Archangel Raphael, sometimes together with Archangel Michael, Uriel, Gabriel and other Ascended Masters such as Mother Mary, Quan Yin, Hilarion, St. Germain and others to come forth and give healing energy to the recipients.

Of Raphael, the *Law of Life* book states: *"Raphael is the Archangel of consecration and concentration. His is the office of dedication. He gives God-assistance to life streams who have dedicated themselves to service to mankind and to world mission. His action is that of concentration. His twin ray is Mary, Mother of Jesus"* (p. 291).

Mother Mary invariably calls upon Archangel Raphael in her discourses. Raphael stands in front of the person and Mother Mary herself stands behind, both beaming light to the client in the middle. Depending on the nature of the healing, she might call upon Raphael for healing and Michael for removal of cords and release of karma. Archangel Raphael and Michael work together to help humankind out of the pain of physicality. It seems to me that the Masters are calling Archangel Raphael more and more often to bring emotional healing and to release pain from humankind, whether physical, emotional or mental.

You can do this too. Call upon Archangel Raphael every night before you go to sleep, and ask that all the healing necessary and beneficial be administered to you during your sleep and continue into the following day for as long as necessary. Ask for the release of physical, emotional, mental, spiritual pain and pollution from your body and from your being in all your body systems, in all times and in all dimensions of reality. Repeat this every night for at least 22 nights. You may have amazing results. Anything that is repeated for 22 consecutive days is mastered. Once mastered, it becomes part of your structure, and it automatically repeats itself. It never hurts to continue longer than that because the mind can (and sometimes does) interfere with the process.

Healing on the Forgiveness Bridge

Commentary: This is a healing given by Archangel Raphael to someone who had been physically abused as a child. The Masters have chosen it to be included here as it has benefits for all. By the mere fact that we are in human embodiment, we have experienced some form of abuse in one lifetime or another. You may want to say, "*I receive this healing and ask that it be applied to all the pain and abuse that I have ever suffered in this and all other lifetimes, past present and future.*" You are invited to receive this healing and adapt it to your own personal needs and experiences.

ARCHANGEL RAPHAEL, CHANNELED DECEMBER 18, 2004

Beloveds, I am Raphael. Take a moment to feel my energy.

Take the palm of your right hand, place it over your heart and breathe into your heart. Close your eyes and focus your attention on your third eye center, the space between your eyebrows. I will send you the image of an angelic presence. You may remember this as my presence. Focus your energy upon the light which I am sending you through your third eye and through the palm of your own hand into your heart. Know that you are protected from all harm.

Know that this is my sign to you. Any time that you sit to meditate with me, close your eyes, place the palm of your right hand on your heart and call upon me: *"Archangel Raphael, I am ready for you. Come to me."* Focus your energy in the center point between your eyebrows and begin to feel my presence and receive my vibration of light through pearlescent and beautiful blue colors, which are also the colors of the robes that Mother Mary is depicted wearing.

It has been described that Mother Mary and Archangel Raphael are of the same angelic lineage. It means that Mother Mary is from the lineage of light which ascends to the angelic realm of Raphael and the legions of Raphael. In our love for humanity, Raphael and Mother Mary chose to come together in human form. Mary in female embodiment came to be the queenly presence on Earth that would bring forth the angelic qualities of love and healing, compassion and forgiveness. She is sitting on an altar, the altar of your heart, within the palace of your own heart. And now, I am asking Mother Mary to emanate to you the colors of pink which you may be feeling or seeing as we speak. If you wish to receive, say, *"Yes. I receive from Mother Mary the emanations of the pink Ray of Divine Love for the healing of all abuse — past, present and future."*

The pink is emanating to you. These are the energies of the love vibration from the heart of Mary. I want to tell you that just as Mary came to Earth to bring the purity of her essence, the purity of her light and love to this Earth, you have come to Earth to bring the purity of your essence and love of your own heart and your own lineage (which goes to Archangel Raphael) to Earth. (Note: this sentence is addressed to those souls whose lineage of light is the same as Mother Mary and Archangel Raphael.)

I have come to tell you that your love has no boundaries. I have come to tell you that I am so well-pleased with you. I have come to tell you that Mother Mary is bathing you in the love that she feels for you. Even when you were a little child, you always said, "I want to help people. I want to heal people. I want to touch people. I want to make people feel good about themselves." You are the one who always tries to make everyone else feel good.

Now as I speak with you, I have changed the colors to emerald green. And this emerald green is the color of the twin flames. I send this emerald green to your heart, and its purpose is to open your energy field to receive and experience happy and healthy relationships.

You have had great hardship in the area of relationships. My dear child, it is not because you do not have love. It is because you have so much love that it will melt the heart with its glory. It is because you have offered your love so abundantly that people become fearful of opening themselves to you. They fear that they may melt in the glow, in the light of this wide open heart of yours. And I promise you that the time will come when you will find the right and nurturing relationships, after I help you to heal your heartache.

Take a moment to breathe deeply and feel the healing of the Emerald Green Ray emanations on your body. It is important for you to see that sometimes the person that you pull to yourself becomes your mirror because you need to heal yourself from the energy that either ignores you or brings fear to your heart. I want you to go into that fear energy. Bring those feelings of fearfulness from the past to the surface. Through remembering the incidents in the past (if you can), they will come to the surface of your energy field, and I will bring you healing by clearing and removing the pain.

Think of any fear that you have been holding inside from the past or present. Let it come to the surface and be washed away with the healing emanations that Archangel Raphael is sending to you.

The energies now are having a deeper purple color with streaks of green; deep dark green. This dark green is to annihilate and to transmute the pain of fear. This is a jade green color. Hold on to this green and know that I am pulling out that fearful energy which was embedded in your cell structure. Take a deep breath and pause for a moment, visualizing the pain fully released.

The energy of violence is held in the first, second and third chakras. Violence is not a heart-based energy, but it is a power-based energy. The energy of it is stored in the stomach area. It is also a survival-based energy. It gathers in the genital area energetically. It is an energy of lack of security and safety. Therefore, it is connected to the root chakra. The fear, insecurity and force of violence and abuse gathers in the three lower chakras. I wish to release this energy from your physical body as well as your mental and emotional bodies

119

What I am saying is that the energy of abuse is held in those areas, just as fear is held in the kidneys and grief in the lungs, just as fear of facing the world translates into migraine headaches. Fear of being unsafe in your environment manifests as sinus infection. Stress comes out as influenza. Catching a flu is a way for the body to say, "I can not cope." That is a short-term, short-lived stress. A body that has become cancerous has gone through a long period of stressful behavior — anger turned within, grief turned within, fear turned within — those energies can turn into cancer. These are the root causes of different ailments. Chinese medicine is so successful because the physical body is not the main focus. The energy body, the Chi body, is addressed. I am, therefore, clearing your energy body.

You may visualize a dark energy over your heart. It may feel like black tar or soot sitting on your heart. Begin to feel it. When you have it in focus, I am going to pull it out. (If you are unable to see or focus on any dark energy, simply intend that whatever may be there is pulled out by Mother Mary.) I will send you a Ruby Red Ray of light. It is a deep maroon, ruby red color. It is very, very deep and dense. It has to be deep and dense and penetrating to be able to take this darkness away from your heart. Begin to visualize the maroon red color. Pause and focus on visualizing the darkness being lifted completely and lightness replacing it.

Now I send you an aquamarine light to replace the vacuum that is left behind from the release of that pain. I ask you to imagine you are on a forgiveness bridge. It is a beautiful bridge, made of orange colored marble. It has a very nice vibration to it. Imagine standing on top of that bridge. When you look to your left, imagine seeing beautiful green colored light, as though it is springtime. There are trees with baby green leaves on them. And when you look to your right, imagine seeing a body of water winding down with a rumbling sound.

Can you bring yourself to invite, one by one, everyone who has caused you pain to come onto this bridge? Pause for a moment and call them on this bridge. As each one comes up, say out loud (or in silence if you are in a public place) whatever you wish to say to each, and then say, "*I am willing to forgive you. I am working on forgiving you.*" If you really feel it in your heart that you can do it, then say "*I do forgive you; I put you in the light and let you go.*"

Your little inner child needs to know that the purpose of this healing is to heal yourself. We want to heal your inner child so that she/he would become a healthy child and would allow you to be a healthy adult. In the process of forgiveness, all others in your life who receive forgiveness can also be freed from the pain they have caused you.

The foremost intention here is to free you from the pain. Also, that you would not read abuse into every man/woman that you pull into your own energy field but that you would emanate to them the love from your heart, which is very abundant. You would go into a neutral place and accept every man/woman to be loving and nurturing and giving of himself/herself, to be fully there for you.

I am always there for you when you call upon me. I hold you in my love and in my light. I am Archangel Raphael. So it is.

121

Mother Mary's Healing Grid with Archangels Michael and Raphael, Jesus and Mary Magdalene

Commentary: The next two healing meditations have a great serendipitous story behind them. A young indigo soul, Avonne, came for two readings with me. In the first, Mother Mary came and offered her the healing grid with the help of Archangels Raphael, Michael, Masters Jesus and Mary Magdalene. In the second, Archangel Uriel offered the Flame of Inner Light, which is the divine spark from the heart of God, The Undifferentiated Source.

In addition to the healing grid, in this exercise Mother Mary also teaches us how to release the pain of Mother Earth when we feel the sorrow of different lands and how to leave our blessings in the air, to benefit those who pass by later. To put this into practical terms, we can offer healing to Mother Earth and all souls who touch that space while waiting in line, sitting in traffic or walking to the office. All it takes is conscious remembrance.

Along with the gift of the healing grid, Mother Mary also asked Avonne to say the Prayer of the Rosary every day while focusing on the picture of the sacred heart of Mary. When Avonne asked, "Which picture of you?" Mother Mary said, "You will know." Avonne went on vacation to New York the following day. While there she went to a church in search of a set of rosary beads to recite the Prayer of the Rosary as Mother Mary had instructed her. While she was paying at the register, her phone rang. It was her bank manager informing her that a check which had been accidentally posted to someone else's account one year ago was now posted safely in her account. The amount? More than $400! As she was pondering on the meaning of this message, her gaze fell upon a printed icon of Mother Mary. Her whole heart lit up as she realized Mother Mary was providing her with a sign and the money to buy the print and the rosary beads. She only noticed later that it was a picture of the Sacred Heart of Mary.

Avonne called me excitedly with this news while I was looking at a shelf full of Quan Yin statues at the oriental market in Houston. I took her call as a sign and purchased the Quan Yin statue I was looking at when she called. Back at home, she placed her Mother Mary picture on her bedroom altar and repeated her healing meditation which Mother Mary had given her, followed by the Prayer of the Rosary.

The following week she came for the second reading. This time Archangel Uriel came to speak with her. Uriel gave her the Flame of Inner Light and asked her to focus on the flame every night during her meditation for the next seven nights. Inspired by her reading, she decided to take photographs of Mother Mary for her altar at home later that day. She took two photos of Mother's icon from the same spot, one after the other. At night she started her meditation by visualizing the Flame of Inner Light given by Archangel Uriel and went on to visualize the meditation with Mother Mary. She envisioned placing Mary Magdalene in front of her, Jesus to her left, Archangel Michael to her right and Mother Mary hovering over her head. She visualized the healing energy that night entering her heart and moving up to her head, chakra by chakra. Then she said her Prayer of the Rosary.

The next morning after her meditation, she decided to take another photo of the Mother Mary icon before she took it to be developed. This time I got an excited call from her after the pictures were developed. The first picture she took came out with a bubble of light coming from Mother Mary's right hand. The second picture showed the bubble of light emanating from Mother's heart chakra right over the sacred heart. The third picture taken the following day (after two sessions of meditation exercises of moving the light from her own heart to her head) showed the bubble of light sitting right at the top of Mother Mary's head at her crown chakra. The head is tilted in Mother's picture yet the bubble of light is still sitting exactly at the top of her head. The Inner Light had traveled to Mother Mary's head, and she was showing Avonne that everything she had done was received and that the light was emanating from Mother Mary herself.

Avonne brought me copies of the photos from the printing shop. When I looked at the pictures, chills ran up my spine and goose-bumps started all over my body. Tears began to run down my face. The feeling of peace that permeated Mother's pictures felt exactly like the energy I had felt on my visits to her apparition sites at Lourdes, Medjegoria, Fatima and even at Milton Hospital in Milton, Massachusetts. Such is the love of the Masters for us. Archangel Uriel's Inner Light and the healing energies are emanating from Mother's heart and head. These two meditation grids are presented below. (You will find these photos of Mother Mary on my website.)

MOTHER MARY, CHANNELED JULY 7, 2004

My beloved children, I am your Mother Mary.

Take a deep breath with me and focus your energy in the center of your heart chakra in the middle of your chest. I will be sending you pink energy. I will call Archangel Raphael to stand behind you and send you energies of pink and gold. I will call Mary Magdalene to stand directly in front of your heart and send you golden pink energy. Open your heart and receive these energies. Remember that I love you and that I will be protecting you and guiding you. Many important events will be coming up for you. At the same time that these important events are happening in your life — in your external life, in this mundane world — there will be a revolution happening inside of you. It will be a revolution of moving into higher Light and of being initiated into this higher Light. Breathe the pink, gold and golden pink energies into your heart. Feel the love that the Masters have for you.

I now call to my son Master Jesus and to Archangel Michael. I ask that my son will stand to your left and Archangel Michael will stand to your right. Mary Magdalene is standing facing you. Archangel Raphael is behind you. I am hovering above you. Remember this formation of Light.

Archangel Raphael is behind you with her arms stretched out. From her heart and from the palms of her hands, she is sending you golden pink light. Mary Magdalene is standing facing you. From her heart and from her third eye, she sends a beam of light to your heart and to your third eye. She holds the palms of your hands in the palms of her hands. The palms of your hands will begin to feel heat, and so will your heart. You may have a tingling sensation or have the feeling of heat moving in your third eye. You may have a feeling of itchiness or pressure on top of your head. The lotus on top of your head is opening up. You may feel as though something is slipping or moving on top of your head.

Every morning when you wake up, call upon your Mother Mary, Mary Magdalene, Archangel Michael, Master Jesus and Archangel Raphael, and ask us to stand around you in this formation. Visualize this formation every day, and remember it frequently during the day to make it stronger. See the golden pink move through you stronger. You already have the golden shield of Archangel Michael. It will give you the protection that you need, and it will also keep you in love (The golden shield of Archangel Michael is the cocoon of 24-Karat gold that sits over your body all the time, given in the Cocoon of Protection meditation.)

All you need to do in the morning is to envision this formation around you, and ask Archangel Michael to magnify the shield of protection around you. In that way, you will have the protection that Archangel Michael brings you as well as the healing strength that this exercise brings.

At night, when you go to sleep, call upon Mary Magdalene and Master Jesus and ask them to take you to their retreat in France to teach you in the Temples of Wisdom. These are etheric temples in the higher realms. Over St. Michel Cathedral in Normandy, France, there is a vortex of energy and an etheric retreat where Master Jesus, Mary Magdalene and Archangel Michael work. I myself and Archangel Raphael bring healing there. I work very closely with Archangel Raphael to bring healing. From that retreat we will teach you.

When you awaken in the morning, you may remember that you have been with us. When you recollect the memory of such events and the teachings, write or tape the memories. You may begin to have lucid dreams. It is as though it is happening consciously. There will be a time where there will be no difference between having visions while you are conscious and while you are dreaming. Your world can become so vivid that you may be able to see events with much greater clarity.

Some of these events may not be pleasant. If you go to different parts of the world, you may become aware of the bloodshed, the wars, the pain and the suffering from lands or people. It is coming to you because it needs to be released. When you see such events, ask Archangel Michael to release the pain from this land and from the people. It is not necessary for you to take the pain into your body.

It is important to make your shield stronger and ask Archangel Michael to create a vortex of light to release the pain from those lands and from the bodies of the people. Call upon their Higher Selves and their souls to give them light and to help them release their pain. Their Higher Selves and their souls, through you, can receive help. Through your prayers and through your light, they can change the darkness that they have absorbed unto themselves and bring it into the light, asking for their mistakes to be released. The pain has to be released in order to anchor the light and love. To release the pain, someone has to agree to release it; somehow, somewhere. I am asking you to pray for this release.

In the meantime, be aware that you have the shield and the protection. With the shield and with the help from Archangel Michael and Jesus, Mary Magdalene, Archangel Raphael and myself, there is much that you can do for people. You do not even need to ask their permission. **Light does not need permission to shine.** If light needed permission to shine, then the Sun would have to ask everyday of all the planets in the solar system, "Can I give you life today?" When you give of yourself without expectation of return, when you give of your light with the help of the Masters, using your body as the catalyst, then you do not have to ask permission. If they wish to receive the healing, they will. If they do not wish to receive it, it will stay in the air; it will bless all the elements, it will bless the Earth. It will bless anyone who passes by, and anyone who is receptive will receive it.

In the presence of light and love, I am your Mother Mary. So it is.

Uriel's Divine Spark of Inner Light

Commentary: In this discourse, Archangel Uriel offers the flame of inner light; the divine spark from the heart of God, the Undifferentiated Source. Uriel is the Guardian of the Inner Light. Sophie Burnham, author of *A Book of Angels*, says of Archangel Uriel, "Uriel brings the light of knowledge of God to men. He is the interpreter of prophecies, the Angel of Retribution. His name means Light of God" (p. 102). He asks us to practice this for a minimum of seven days.

URIEL, CHANNELED JULY 20, 2004

My beloved, I am Uriel.

I have come to you because I wish to give you the light from my own heart. Uriel is the holder of the Inner Light, divine spark from the heart of God. I have come to offer you that inner spark. Within one week from today your energies will be increased dramatically. I want you to receive the higher energies and allow them to be filtered into your heart. As they enter your heart, I want to make sure that they move through your heart into the flame that I will place in the center of your heart. This flame will protect you from lower energies and it will raise your vibration to a much higher one. From today, you have seven days for this flame to establish itself inside your heart. When new energies begin to pour down to Earth, you will be in a good position to absorb them, to digest them and to raise your own vibration accordingly.

But before I do that, I want to ask your permission to place the flame inside your heart. The name of this flame is the Inner Divine Spark of Light from the Heart of God. This flame was given to me when God decided to feel Itself in many bodies and many forms. This Divine Spark was hidden inside the Heart of God. God allowed me to take this Divine Spark and bring it to the surface of existence. Then I offered this Divine Spark to Metatron, the Archangel who has created with this Spark all of creation. When I handed this spark to Metatron, it moved from being the inner spark to becoming the outer spark. With the outer spark externalized, Metatron created everything in this universe.

Five sacred geometric symbols were involved in the creation. But more important than those is this spark. In the universe, everyone functions because of the outer spark. For humanity to return to God Unity and know that the spark of God is in their own heart, they have to reignite this inner spark in their own hearts. God has given me the dispensation to ignite the inner spark. This is the first time that I come to return this inner spark to the heart of humanity.

Take a deep breath. Feel my presence in front of you. I am a very tall angel. I am a very powerful angel. I have a lot of strength and stamina. And yet, I do not belong to this world of yours, so my energy is very etheric. Whereas Archangel Michael's energy (because he has been here on Earth helping humanity) has become very strong and very grounded, my energy is very other-worldly. You may feel as though a cloud is coming around you. You may feel the warmth. You will feel my energy differently from the energy of Archangel Michael. When Archangel Michael comes, you know immediately because his energy is strong and it grounds you. You have come to know the protection that he brings. My energy is more of a feminine force. It relates to the creative forces. It is very light. It would be like a gentle breeze. It would be a gentle warmth in your heart. You may begin feeling a bright white, gold and yellow light that will be coming to your face, to your heart, to your throat, feeling it in your shoulders, feeling it even in the palms of your hands. Pause and feel the sensation.

Now I will place my right hand into my own heart. From my own heart I will bring out the spark of the inner light and I will give that spark to you. And I will place it right in the center of your chest above your lungs, between your shoulder blades. It is between your heart chakra and your throat chakra. This is the center that we call the cosmic heart. This is where I will place it because this spark is the spark of light from the cosmic heart of God. And with this spark of light, I ignite your own cosmic heart.

As you awaken every morning, think of Archangel Uriel as you focus your energy on seeing this spark in your own heart. It is fine if you wish to see it inside your own personal heart, but it is also fine for you to see it in your cosmic heart between your heart chakra in the middle of your chest and your throat chakra. Focus on it so that it becomes strengthened. From today, for seven days it is important that you connect to this flame every day (or night) to strengthen it and to help me make it brighter for you. When you focus on Uriel and the energy of the spark in your heart, that is when you give me permission to ignite it and make it bigger. At the end of the seven days, this light will be much brighter in your heart. This light will remind you of your divinity and help you to walk on the path of your divine mission that you have come to Earth to accomplish.

The three months ahead of us (August, September, October 2005) are very important times for Earth and humanity. Some of you have been prepared for many hundreds of thousands of years to face this time and to help others to raise their vibration and feel the light. Some people are still sleeping; they do not even know that the Divine Spark is going to be ignited in their hearts. This is why those of you who are aware of it are now actively working with us. This is why we have to work harder together to help those who are still asleep awaken to their divinity. **All of you become the beacons of light.**

You would be a transmitter of this light. Wherever you go, the energy around you will be conducive to people receiving it. Even when you are in a supermarket or a movie theater, everybody else who is in that space has the opportunity to receive the Divine Spark. It is as though a seed has been planted inside of you. And in a very short time, it becomes a fruit-bearing tree. And the tree will give its fruits, and you can hand the fruits to everyone that is passing by. In a matter of an instant the seed that has been planted in your heart becomes a fruit-bearing tree, and the tree will give ripe fruits. And eating the ripe fruits will benefit everyone just as will the seed that was planted in your heart.

Take a deep breath with me. Feel the warmth around your body and the spark in your heart until it is fully established. Remember me for the next seven days. To increase the Divine Spark, you can say with me now: *"Archangel Uriel, I ask you to come every day and ignite this Divine Spark for the next seven days in my heart. I offer what I receive in service to all humankind and for the benefit of light. I ask that this Divine Spark will help me walk on my path of my divine mission. I ask that the doors of light be opened to me and that I can see and feel the presence of the Masters and the angelic forces of light with me and around me. I ask that I can hear their guidance and assistance, their verbal communication and the visual perception that they send me in the light of the I AM THAT I AM. I ask that my visual perception of the Masters and their guidance be increased. I ask that my ability to communicate verbally with the Masters and Angels of Light be increased. I ask all the obstacles to be released so that I can directly hear and see Masters of Light, Angels of Light, Great Beings of Light and the presence of God with me, around me, ahead of me, behind me in every particle of life. So it is. It is done. Amen.*

I love you from the core of my heart. I am Uriel.

Part Three ~ Manifestation

Introduction to Manifestation, Thoth and Quan Yin

One of the important facets of spiritual evolution is power to manifest. Manifestation at its highest potential becomes "precipitation" or "instant precipitation." This is the power to manifest, as though from thin air, the objects of one's desire or the intentions to further a cause. Many of the Ascended Masters of Light, such as St. Germain, Metatron, Quan Yin and Thoth are known for their qualities and abilities of precipitation or instant manifestation. The process is an alchemical one where the Master holds the five elements of Earth, Water, Fire, Air and Ether at their command and materializes objects of intentions from the higher realms into this reality. Therefore the analogy of manifesting from thin air is in fact correct to some extent.

A contemporary living saint who is the Master of Instant Manifestation is Sathya Sai Baba. A holy man born in India who manifests in his hands objects — jewelry made of gold and silver and precious gems — which he gives to people who come to visit him. He also manifests a powder-like substance — a sacred ash called "vibuti" — which has great healing powers. Vibuti can be used for healing by rubbing on the body for physical, mental, emotional and spiritual healing. Small quantities of vibuti can be taken orally as well. Sai Baba says to his disciples. "When you come to me, I give you what you want, in the hope that someday you will want what I am here to give you."

What he is here to give us is spiritual evolution and empowerment to attain Mastery. Once we become Masters of our own bodies, lives and destinies, his work is done. He can then be freed from bondage to this limited body of matter and leave Earth and all that it holds to live in the bliss of the I AM in the higher dimensions of Light where he belongs. Until we get to those levels, however, he patiently receives thousands of devotees who visit his ashrams (holy abodes) in India. He tirelessly gives his love and light and the gifts he manifests from the higher realms in order to empower humanity, Earth and the five elements to reach and grow to Mastery.

He has promised to remain on Earth into his nineties and then return for another embodiment as Prema Sai, bestower of Love. The name he has chosen for his present embodiment is Sathya Sai, bestower of truth. He had come to Earth before this in one previous embodiment. He is known from that lifetime as Sai Baba of Shiridi. Baba is a familiar name denoting father. He is one of the contemporary spiritual fathers and Masters of our time. I have given an account of Sathya Sai in my first *Gifts* book, *Gifts from the Ascended Beings of Light*. Books on the miracles and teachings of Sai Baba are available practically throughout the world and are becoming ever more popular. Translations of his teachings, as well as people's accounts of their life-changing stories, are available from spiritual stores in many languages.

A brief collection of his words of wisdom are posted daily on a blackboard in his ashrams in India. On one of my visits to his ashram, I read the day's message. In it, he had made a reference to the state of the world. He stated that this world was bound to continue and succeed in its evolution because he had taken physical embodiment. He said, "There will be no failures, because I am here." He has come to Earth, therefore Earth must continue to evolve without any failures. He has come to manifest the continuation and succession of many generations of human beings yet to come to Earth in future eons of time. Inside his ashrams, the essence of instant manifestation is tangible. Even outside the ashram, his presence and his powers of manifestation and precipitation continue to work in the lives of people he has touched. When you receive him by calling him into your life, you can feel his presence in your life and the lives of those you touch in tangible ways.

My own first experience of his presence and his power was when I hugged a friend who had recently returned from visiting Sathya Sai Baba's ashram in India. As soon as our bodies touched in the embrace I felt Sathya Sai Baba's presence, and I immediately had to sit down to meditate with him. He had no time to waste. In that meditation he gave me the dates for my visits to India and the length of time for my stay. He told me it was imperative that I visit him during that time.

When I arrived, I received a private interview with him. In that interview, he manifested before my own eyes vibuti ashes which he poured into a mound in the palm of my hands. He manifested two beautiful rings for two other people who were in that interview room. He offered great love and compassion to everyone. Through his humility, he acted as though we were doing him a favor to be in his presence. Ascended Masters of Light are also capable of performing great feats of instant manifestation and miracles. Some of the teachings that are given here are examples of ways to achieve these feats through their teachings in our personal lives.

Alchemy is the art and the science of turning base metal into gold. It is a physical science where the Master actually changes base metal to gold. It is also an art and a mystery where the metaphor of turning base metal to gold is applied in which the novice student of the occult grows to become a Master of Wisdom. The metaphor also applies to an unawakened soul whose wisdom and understanding is the equivalent of base metal; once awakened to the knowledge of its own divinity, the soul becomes pure. Then the gold quality of the soul begins to shine forth. In awakening to the presence of the soul and its pure nature, a human being can move from the stage of base metal to that of pure gold, or from ape-man to Hu-mankind (Hu is one of the ancient names of God).

There are many phases in the manifestation process whether you apply the process at soul level or at the level or personality. The soul will awaken to the Divine Spark and learn to manifest its potential as a Master. Ultimately with practice, the soul will merge into spirit and manifest its full potential as a self-realized or enlightened being. Through the process of realizing the Self, the soul attains Mastery. This in essence is one aspect of turning the base metal into gold.

The personality, on the other hand, is in charge of mundane aspects of a human being's life. The personality too evolves through the process of manifestation. As a human being, the personality identifies with the world first by living a life of survival. Its needs are basic: food, shelter and clothing. As the personality grows, it evolves from survival and basic needs to greater wisdom through maturing, knowledge and education. With growth in these fields, the personality's expectation from life changes. The needs become more complex as the personality matures to expect levels of comfort and service that are above and beyond basic needs. With growth through every level of evolution to greater complexities, the personality develops higher expectations of itself and of its environment. With that comes responsibility.

The cave people's only responsibilities were to survive the harsh environment, and there was very little damage that the cave people could do to their environment. At that time, it was the environment which was harsh and unkind to humankind. Now that is reversed, and humankind is harsh and unkind to the environment. Today, people of the civilized world are responsible for much greater problems as well as for feats of achievement. Even survival in today's modern world takes a different meaning. As the world evolves and the people begin to face their responsibilities, a point is reached where humankind gains the maturity and the wisdom to serve, nurture, nourish and share. Service to each other, to the planet and to all of God's creation becomes the utmost goal of life. That is when the personality moves from the base metal (the cave people) to gold (people of one world sharing all the resources and rebuilding Earth together). The examples of such people are beings such as Sathya Sai Baba and other spiritual living Masters and teachers who have devoted their lives in service to humankind. Theirs is the pure gold nugget of 24-Karat gold. The personality is immersed in the soul and the soul in the spirit. The Ascended Masters are also the gold nuggets. They share their wisdom with us freely, and they offer their service for our benefit. They work for the growth and maturity of all souls, the planet and Mother Earth herself. They continue to serve ceaselessly for the greater good of all.

The purpose of this section and the teachings of the Masters on the subject of manifestation is to raise the vibration of our souls and our personalities to higher levels. At such levels of Light, we can enter the realm of instant manifestation or precipitation at will while we are still in physical embodiment.

None of the exercises that follow can bring you instant manifestation right away. But they all can bring you the awareness that you have the power to manifest the object of your desires from the unlimited resources of the world. Then they can help you to exercise the powers which are your divine right to achieve and to practice until you have perfected them. In the process, you gain power. Once you have matured to that perfection, then Mastery and instant manifestation move within the realms of possibility and come into the range of your abilities. At that point, it becomes important to use these powers to benefit all and to share and distribute the resources. For as long as we use the power and the resources for our personal benefits and against the benefit of all, we will not mature to levels of Mastery, and obstacles will arise before us.

When we do finally reach those levels, the joy and bliss of serving and sharing is unlimited and makes the process worthwhile. In the exercises that follow, I have chosen manifestation techniques and empowerment tools from Master Thoth the Atlantean, who ascended Earth over 25,000 years ago. For thousands of years before that, he brought the secrets of alchemy and instant manifestation for anchoring on Earth through many civilizations during the Lemurian and Atlantean times. Thoth is responsible for creation of all the spoken and written languages of Earth.

He has been especially involved in rescuing the knowledge and wisdom from Atlantis before its destruction. He was instrumental in reseeding the Atlantean wisdom into the civilizations which became Egypt (Land of Khem, or Chen, where the secrets of alchemy were brought) as well as into the Mayan and Aztec civilizations. I have given extensive descriptions of Master Thoth in *Gifts III*.

Emerald Tablets is a great legacy left by Thoth for humankind. It consists of fourteen emerald green tablets made of an indestructible material:

> "...*formed from a substance created through alchemical transmutation, upon which Thoth had inscribed the knowledge of the mysteries of the universe and the cosmic laws governing all bodies of matter, including our own bodies and Mother Earth. Also knowledge of how to conquer all that is in matter or form and move beyond it into immortality" (Doreal, p. ii).*

Doreal, who translated the original inscriptions of the Emerald Tablets, has compiled them into a book called *The Emerald Tablets of Thoth the Atlantean*. He states that they date back to 36,000 years before Christ, and their original author was called Thoth, the Atlantean priest king. He founded a colony in Egypt after the Atlantean continent sank. He built the pyramids of Giza and inside them stored the wisdom and hid the knowledge of the mysteries which he had brought from Atlantis:

> "*For some 16,000 years, he ruled the ancient race of Egypt, from approximately 50,000 B.C. to 36,000 B.C. At that time, the ancient barbarous race among which he and his followers had settled had been raised to a higher degree of civilization. Thoth was an immortal,*

that is, he had conquered death, passing only when he willed and even then not through death. His vast wisdom made him ruler over the various Atlantean colonies, including the ones in South and Central America.

When the time came for him to leave Egypt, he erected the Great Pyramid over the entrance to the Great Halls of Amenti, placed in it his records, and appointed guards for his secrets from among the highest of his people. In later times, the descendants of these guards became the pyramid priests, while Thoth was deified as the God of Wisdom, The Recorder, by those in the age of darkness which followed his passing. In legend, the Halls of Amenti became the underworld, the Halls of the Gods, where the soul passed after death for judgment" (Doreal, p.1).

Thoth himself, having ascended, moved his ego personality through the bodies of humankind and incarnated three more times on Earth in the body, but with intelligence of superhuman nature. The last of the three incarnations, he came as Hermes Trismejistus, "three times glorified" or "three times born." In that lifetime, he left a large body of written materials know as *Hermetica* which is the wisdom of the planetary influences of the signs of zodiac in the body of Earth and in the lives of humankind and how to override these influences. These writings influenced the great thinkers, scientists, artists and philosophers of the world such as Leonardo Da Vinci, Isaac Newton, Roger Bacon, Milton, Boticelli, Thomas More, Paracelsus, Shakespeare, Kepler, Copernicus, Victor Hugo and Carl Jung, as well as Islamic and Jewish philosophers. The esoteric philosophers have equated Thoth and the writings of *Hermetica* to equal the mysterious prophet Enoch and his writings.

Hermetica is considered *"a cornerstone of western culture"* (Freke and Gandy, pp. 7-8). As Thoth, the God of Wisdom, he is believed to have revealed to the Egyptians the knowledge of astronomy, geometry, architecture, medicine, religion and spiritual knowledge and wisdom. In this book, Thoth, through channelings in group workshops, has given us the Emerald Green Sphere of Manifestation and the following segments which are great manifestation tools. Quan Yin and Metatron are two of the other contributing Masters in this section. Metatron is an archangel as well as an Ascended Master, whom I will explain in detail in the Enlightenment section.

Quan Yin is the Goddess of Compassion, an Ascended Master who attained Mastery over 14,000 years ago. She has been greatly involved with the evolution of Earth and humankind, especially the young generations of souls born since 1972 known as the Indigo souls. These are highly evolved souls who are here on Earth to raise the vibration of Earth to higher levels and to help in the awakening of all souls to their divinity and in time to come with the ascension of Earth.

Quan Yin is a Bodhisattva. Also known as Kuan Yin or Kuan Shihi Yin, her name means, "hearer of the cries of the world." She is revered in the East as a great Divine Mother: loving, protective, merciful, compassionate, tender and wise. She comes to the rescue of all her children everywhere. The Bodhisattvas are great individuals who have attained God-realization and have devoted their lives and their souls in service to others. The Bodhisattva vow is that whoever takes it will remain attentive in service and guidance of souls until every soul has achieved God-realizaton or God Unity. Quan Yin's mantra is OM MANI

PADME HUM which means "Hail to the jewel (or pearl) inside the lotus." The lotus is the symbol of spiritual attainment and self-realization; the pearl removes pain. OM MANI PADME HUM is a potent and effective mantra which you can use at all times, especially when you wish to call upon Quan Yin for her guidance and assistance. Another beneficial simple mantra is NAMO AMI TOFO meaning "Hail to the Buddha." A third mantra is "NAMO QUAN SHIH YIN POSA meaning "Hail to the hearer of the cries of the world compassionate one." For more about Quan Yin, read her chapter in *Gifts I*.

Emerald Green Flame of Manifestation in the Heart

Commentary: In this exercise we will work with Master Thoth to receive the green flame of instant manifestation. This flame will be established in the center of the heart chakra. We can place our intentions inside of the flame of instant manifestation and ask it to bring these intentions into our lives. The flame has its own consciousness, supervised by Master Thoth who will help the manifestation process for us, provided that it is in our highest wisdom. He then gives us a gift himself — peace and harmony. He places this gift inside our green flames and asks that we also choose our individual intentions to place inside the green flame along with his gift.

In the section entitled, "Grid of Peace — Our Role as Teachers and Healers," he explains the importance of purifying our hearts and standing in our truth, becoming beacons of light and truth and letting others receive from us through our touch, our words and our teachings. In the section, "Maroon-Magenta Sphere of Light — Lemurian Crystals", he expands the green flame of the heart bigger to hold our entire body within it. He then places a deep maroon-magenta sphere around the green flame over our body. Inside of this sphere he takes us on a journey to the land of Mu, the civilization of Lemuria, to connect with the pillars of the crystalline structure called the selenite crystals. These selenite pillars are huge, clear crystal structures approximately eight to ten feet tall and three to seven feet wide. From there we visit the golden-domed Temple, receiving prosperity from the feminine energies through these encounters. He brings us the memories, activation of the skills and the tools, which we possessed during our lifetimes in Lemuria.

MASTER THOTH, CHANNELED JUNE 3, 2003

Adonai. Adonai. Adonai. I am Thoth. Take a deep breath with me.

Hold focus in an emerald green flame of light in the center of your heart. The diameter of this green light is one and a half inches wide, two and a half inches high. It vibrates emerald green, the Ray of Manifestation, Precipitation, Instant Illumination. Precipitation means instant manifestation.

When you want to bring ideas to reality, a wish or a thought to turn into physical manifest form, take that thought or wish and place it inside of your green flame. See it clearly in your mind's eye. If you don't have a clear idea of what you want or you are not sure what to ask for, then sit in meditation first and ask your master guides or ask me to tell you what would be best for you at this present moment. If you have already placed an intention into the flame, maintain that intention and continue by asking what will be the highest wisdom. Both intentions will be carried forth. Both will manifest should they be in your highest interest.

Take a deep breath and see your intentions placed inside of the green flame. Feel the warmth and the essence of the flame surrounding your intention.

GRID OF PEACE — OUR ROLE AS TEACHERS AND HEALERS

Now I will make an intention on your behalf and give it as a gift to you. I would like to offer to you peace and harmony in the days to come. Peace and harmony to be a pillar of light, an antenna of light. Transmitting through you like a beacon the love and light, peace and harmony that is given to you for your own personal use and to benefit this entire universe.

To make this light brighter, frequently go back to the space of the heart and envision the emerald green flame. In time as you practice, the magical presence of the emerald green Ray of Manifestation will become larger. As the enlargement continues, the peace and harmony that you will feel daily — in spite of all the events that may happen around you — will become greater. People will comment on how beneficial it is to be in your energy, because when you are around they feel peaceful.

I give you this gift. What you do with it is up to you. I will maintain the state of peace and harmony for 36 hours from this moment just to show you its truth and its validity, its reality. You may feel much more peaceful during the next three days than you have felt for a very long time. It will feel like the state of peace that comes after a long meditation.

After this time, activate and recalibrate the flame of emerald green in the center of your heart on a daily basis. You may activate it each time for a 48-hour period. In this way, if you miss it one day, it remains active. For as long as you continue to recalibrate and reactivate the flame daily, or every other day, you will maintain the peace and harmony.

When you lose your peace, go back to it. My offer to you is eternal. This gift I offer you for your commitment to the service of Light.

The dross needs to be cleared from your planet and from the consciousness of all souls. The clearing will move you and your planet to a higher grade of Light and help the spirit to descend upon you, your planet and the consciousness of the masses. My request is that you take the responsibility of teaching others. I am asking you to open yourself to teach and to heal others. You may not call yourself a healer or a teacher, but that does not mean you cannot be one. There will come times when you know you have touched someone. They may not consciously know it. Their dreams, their eating habits and their likes and dislikes will change, their third eye will open up and they will begin to want to live life differently. Then they may find in you an oasis of Light, a great mentor or a teacher. My request is to open your heart and mind to receive these human beacons of Light into your life and your heart. Allow them to come into your life. Allow them to raise their vibration in harmony with your own vibration.

Teach them what they need. Sometimes you teach by putting your hand on someone's head or back, by saying a pleasant word, even by bringing something to someone's attention that they do not want to hear. Have the courage to stand in your own truth and to remove yourself from all bias, lack of self-worth, lack of self-confidence, from being defensive or offensive. Just go into neutral, and express the truth as you see it.

Do not be attached to the fruits of your action. If the action brings up anger, be gentle to yourself first and to the person next. If you have to remove yourself from the situation, do so. You may have to apologize by saying, "I make no apologies for what I have said, but I apologize that it has disturbed you. I still stand in my truth." Do it without fear, do it with abandon (surrender). Do it for the sake of Light, for the sake of truth. **The Emerald Green Ray of Manifestation can be active and can accomplish its highest task only when you stand in your own truth.** Remember that this Emerald Green is the Ray of Truth, it is the Fifth Ray. It is the Ray of Freedom from Bondage and Attainment of Illumination. Five is the number for freedom. Five is the number for change. Welcome the change.

Maroon-Magenta Sphere of Light: Lemurian Crystals

Bring your attention to the energies of the emerald green flame in the heart. The group energy and vibration will continue to spin faster and faster, creating and illuminating a grid around your body. Furthermore, it creates a grid around the planet for all who reach up in vibration of Light to receive the same emerald green flame and to place it in their heart. They may begin to vibrate to these energies by opening their hearts, raising their vibration and even by being in your blessed presence. Envision now that the flame is becoming so big that you are actually standing inside of it.

The flame forms around your entire physical body. I will place a deep maroon-magenta purple colored, shiny sphere of light around the green. This is the highest vibration of divine love from the heartcore of the Undifferentiated Source. I am given a dispensation to offer it to you. Inside of this sphere of light, I will take you to your lifetimes in the civilization you know as the land of Mu, the civilization of Lemuria.

I take you safely from your bodies to that civilization, and your consciousness will become aware of bodies that are larger and much taller than your present physical bodies. You find yourself inside a more masculine body with well-formed muscles. You might find yourself in male or in female bodies. The texture of the skin is much thicker, and the color is darker and deeper. It is an orange, bronze-golden color. Look down at your attire. Look up at the sky and adjust your vision. You may recollect memories of life-times as teachers at the Temples of Wisdom in Lemuria. You worked with pillars of selenite — eight to ten feet tall; three, five or seven feet in diameter. You knew how to directly transmit your energy from your body to the selenite. To teleport yourself inside it, you would vibrate your energy body with the crystals. Those pillars of selenite crystal were your vehicles of Light. They were used for time travel and journeys to other planets.

Look right in front of you. You are standing in front of a huge pillar of selenite crystal, a very tall pillar of clear light crystal formation. (For those of you who are not already in the possession of a piece of selenite, I would highly recommend that you find yourself a piece after this exercise. And even if you acquire a small piece, do so after this session for your own nurturance. You will find that you can connect to the selenite with great ease because of this exercise. It will be of great healing and comfort and a pleasant surprise.)

Begin connecting with the piece of selenite. Send out a beam of light from your third eye, another beam from your solar plexus, and two beams of light one from each palm of your hands. Holding out the palms of your hands touch the piece of selenite, and immediately you are teleported inside of the crystal.

Take a deep breath and get acquainted with the environment. Reconnect with your own power from that time. Ask for a decoding of the memory banks from the Lemurian times. Ask to remember what helps you to walk the path of Light in this lifetime with greater ease and power, wisdom and understanding. Ask for a decoding of the information that will assist your work with Light, to bring with ease all information, tools, resources, abundance, comfort, peace, joy, fun, wisdom and power. Feel your heart fill with the Light and the peace that you always maintained in that lifetime. As you grow and merge into your own power generator selenite pillar crystal, I will begin to form around your body the maroon-magenta sphere of Light. Merged in the Light, we will teleport from here back to the selenite pillar for the journey to visit with feminine principles to receive prosperity and abundance.

Meeting Feminine Principle to Receive Prosperity

Look in front of you. You will see a golden doorway. You are invited to go through this golden doorway and enter the golden-domed Hall of Light. Meet the Feminine

Principle of Existence, Goddess Beings who have offered their bodies as vehicles of Light, illuminating the Earth. Stand before them and receive their illumined Light. Join and merge into their essence, and take a deep breath. Ask this Feminine Essence for a gift. If you have something you wish for, ask it. If you do not, ask them to give you what they choose. If you wish for both, ask for both. On your behalf, I ask the Feminine Principle to bring to you prosperity and abundance, illumination and peace. I ask on your behalf for comfort and luxury, health and wholeness in body, mind, spirit and emotions. I ask the creative forces to bless you and nurture you with every breath, so that you may experience the perfection originally intended by God.

Every day ask for the abundance and prosperity — in emotions, in mind, in physical matter, in resources, in finances, in comfort and in luxury — to open up to you. Ask for success, and bring this quality to Earth allowing others to receive from you. You are the points of a spear with very sharp edges, which makes an arrow of Light. Its destination is the heartcore of the multitudes and masses of humanity and of Mother Earth. **Your mission is to land as a beacon of Light in that central heartcore and to transfer the Light to Earth and to the multitudes and masses of humankind.** Then the Light of God-Unity can breathe the spirit of God into everything it touches.

EMBODIMENT OF THE LEMURIAN SELF

Become aware of the sphere of maroon-magenta purple light forming around you again. Become aware of yourself fully illuminated in golden white light, standing inside of the sphere. Become aware of the emerald green flame which has turned into golden white, illuminating your entire body. We are returning into the pillars of selenite.

Become aware of your physical countenance in your Lemurian body. Reconnect with that body. Ask that being to be your guide, for that being is of a higher elevation of Light than what you have attained so far in this body through this present seed-race. What that seed-race attained, we intend to conquer in this lifetime as we open ourselves to the new seeding of the Seventh Golden Age. To anchor the energies of this Golden Age, you have to attain the highest vibration and retrieve it from the best of the seed races before you.

To receive new tools, you can go back to that body you occupied during the Lemurian civilization. You can call upon this being. Although this being is yourself, the self you were in that lifetime, right now they can play the role of your guide. You may be very familiar with them but have never known this is you in your Lemurian lifetimes. You may have always thought of them as your Higher Self. Now that you have found this aspect of yourself in the higher realms, you can move to the next level with their help. This aspect is now one with you.

Take a deep breath and begin releasing yourself from the Lemurian time. Become aware of your maroon-magenta sphere of Light. See yourself standing inside of the sphere. The emerald green flame is now moving from all around you into the core of your heart. The color is moving from golden white back to emerald green.

The sphere is becoming transparent and it is no longer spinning. You may ask the maroon-magenta sphere to remain around your body. It does not have to spin at all times. In its stationary mode, it will encapsulate all the information and keep you connected to higher realms of consciousness without interference from the outer world.

Let us ask for protection through the blessed presence of Archangel Michael. May the Cosmic Christ Heart-Flame shine within your heart, now and forever.

In your love, I am Thoth. Adonai. Adonai.

Candle Grid for Accomplishing Life's Mission

Commentary: This is an excellent candle grid. Its purpose is to bring all things to its original state of purity and innocence that God intended for humankind. You can set up this grid both for the general overall purpose of accomplishing your life's mission and for specific issues or events that you wish to accomplish. **Any intention that you would want to realize needs to be returned to its state of original purity and innocence before it can be fully accomplished, unless you want to continue struggling in various karmic situations.** Only those intentions which are karmic debts do not originate from a state of purity and innocence. Everything else in God's creation does begin from that state and must return to that state. Therefore, Metatron's exercise here is an excellent manifestation tool. For example, you can use this grid if you are not happy in your job or current career choice. It can be used for business or personal partnerships and transactions, health and wholeness of yourself, of your young or teenage children or of senior parents. It can be used to find loving partners and spouses, to remove obstacles from your path, to release depression, to succeed in career and social life and for anything else you can think of.

Candles are powerful because they represent all the four base elements with which this entire creation was created. When lighted, the flame of the candle represents the element of Fire. The smoke and the air that it needs to remain lighted represent the element of Air. The wax represents both Water and Earth. The color white represents purity and innocence. Originally before we entered into the realms of density and darkness there was only light, and light was represented as Pure White Light. With white candles, Metatron teaches us to reinstate the white light of purity and innocence into our lives. You can use this candle grid for absolutely all your intentions. The idea is to bring that intention to its original state of purity and innocence so that it can manifest in your life in peace and harmony with ease and grace. Simply set your candle grid up as Metatron explains below and say, *"I set up this grid to bring (state your intent) to its original state of purity and innocence and manifest it for my life"* (or release it from my life, whichever is applicable).

METATRON, CHANNELED NOVEMBER 6, 2003

Beloved of my own heart, I am Metatron. Take a deep breath with me.

To accomplish your life's mission, to remember that mission and to walk the path of the Light of your mission, set up a candle grid. This candle grid is for the accomplishment of your life's mission by returning to the purity of the original intent. For this grid you will need to use five white candles, large enough that they would burn for five days. Dedicate each one for one of these qualities: 1) peace, 2) harmony, 3) clarity, 4) joy and 5) light. Set them up around in a circle. In the center, place a container of water, preferably a clear glass container. All around the container of water, sprinkle a dusting of cinnamon. The purpose of the water is to clear the path from all obstacles and to cleanse your emotional body. It represents the element of Water. The purpose of cinnamon is to absorb to itself the objects of your desires. It represents the element of Earth. The purpose of the candle flame is to bring the fire of passion and compassion to your intentions. The flame represents the element of Fire, and the flame cannot exist unless the element of Air gives it wind, gives it wings to fly. The element of air is represented everywhere in your grid.

With the help of the air, the illumined flame will take wings and take all your intentions to the heart of God, the Source of All That Is, in the Ether which is the fifth and final element holding within itself all the other elements. All the thoughtforms that have ever existed are held in the element of Ether. The object of this candle grid is to pick from those thoughtforms in the mind of God the ones that will best serve you on the journey of your divine mission and the accomplishment of it; whether you will best serve by healing, teaching, serving humankind or serving the Light in any other way possible.

Set up the grid, place the five candles, say out loud the quality of each candle and the intentions for each: peace, harmony, clarity, joy and light. Light each one and sit with it for a few minutes. Envision a blue ball of Light in the base of your spine. Begin to move the ball upwards from the base of your spine, chakra by chakra, along your spinal column to the top of your head. Begin envisioning the presence of your primary guide and your guardian angel behind you. Pause and meditate, feeling the energies. From the very point of coming to existence, you have a hierarchy of guardian angels. Archangel Michael and Lady Faith have come to rescue humanity from forgetfulness of their divinity. Call upon them and ask them to help you in the remembrance of who you are and what you have come to do on Earth. Ask the Light from the heartcore of God — the Undifferentiated Source — to shine upon this grid, your body and your Being, your loved ones, your home, all of your possessions, those that you will touch, that you have touched and that you have been touched by, and upon those that will clear the path for you to serve as you clear the path for others to serve the Light. Pray and meditate, and ask over and over: *"Not my will, but thy will be done. I surrender to your will. I surrender to the Light, the pure, bright white light of the Source, I walk on the path of Light accomplishing my mission and I ask for divine power, divine wisdom and divine love to engulf me now and forever. So it is. It is done. Amen."*

Say these prayers. Sit with your candle. Meditate. Your life is changing from moment to moment. A week from today you may feel much greater strength, love and hope within yourself and in your life.

In the Light of the I AM, I am your own Metatron. So it is.

155

Mantra for Manifestation of New Ideas and Accomplishments

Commentary: Metatron's intention for these mantras is to raise the vibration of our body and being for the awakening of the masses of humanity and for our spiritual growth as well as for the growth of Mother Earth. Metatron gave this discourse after Thanksgiving in 2002 when many portals of Light had opened up to Earth and to humankind. Important planetary events were in progress, which had begun in August of 2002. Metatron is beckoning us to take advantage of the manifestation portals that have opened up since August of 2002 and to call new ideas, designs and accomplishments to come forth to us. He is preparing us through the recitation of these mantras to open our own channels of Light to receive these ideas and to accomplish them in service to the Light and on behalf of the Masters to benefit Earth and humankind.

Metatron and other Masters have told us in many channelings that when humanity reaches a certain level of development, ideas and designs are floated to Earth's atmosphere for absorption. Those human beings who are open can then receive and use those ideas and turn them into inventions, services and accomplishments to benefit Earth and humankind. This is why sometimes two or three people in two different corners of the world come up with the same idea. The idea is given to humankind by the Masters as they see our world and humanity ready to receive and use them in beneficial ways. When we say the following mantras, we open ourselves to receive the ideas, and we announce to the Masters and higher realms our willingness to put these ideas into good use on behalf of the world in service to the Light.

METATRON, CHANNELED NOVEMBER 29, 2002

Beloved of my own heart, I am Metatron. Take a deep breath with me.

Bring your attention to serving the Light and intend that you will use all that you receive for the benefit of all. Visualize yourself in receptive mode. See that the pathways are open for you to enter, the same pathways that have been blocked until this moment. When you are open, you can change the world to make it a better place. **It is in the middle of chaos that you find the greatest peace.** Find your own peace. It is in the middle of chaos that greatest inventions are made, the greatest creations are brought to the surface, the greatest of attainments and achievements are attained and achieved. Remember this mantra and repeat it over and over:

I AM the mind of God. I AM the heart of God.
I now bring forth from the mind of God ideas and accomplishments,
which have never been brought forth or accomplished before.
I now bring forth from the heart of God
the Light and love that purifies Earth and all souls.

Make this your daily mantra. Make this your resonant sound. Let every breath bring you the memory that:
I AM the heart of God and I AM the mind of God.
I AM returning to my pure and divine origin.
I AM is my divine right. I AM is my pure light.
I AM is my original blueprint.
I AM the life and the resurrection.

When you say this one mantra, you embody yourself with illumination of the I AM THAT I AM. You bring forth life in the purest and most innocent essence. You bring the divinity of the Godhead into your body. You embody that divinity. When you speak of the resurrection, you speak of your own knowing and remembrance that you are that life, that you are that God, that you are the divine embodied.

With great love, I stand at your feet as your humble servant, Metatron. So it is.

I AM the Resurrection and the Life

Commentary: In many different readings and discourses, Metatron asks people to repeat Master Jesus' saying "I Am the resurrection and the Life" (John 11:25). In *Gifts I (Gifts from Ascended Beings of Light: Prayers, Meditations, Mantras, and Journeys for Soul Growth)*, there is a discourse in which Metatron explains this mantra. He calls it the first and last mantra. Here he asks that we repeat both aspects of it:

I am the resurrection and the life.
I am the life and the resurrection.

Many times when I am in the middle of a channeling session I can see the world through that higher power, and I fully understand the higher truth. After a while when I return back to my contracted, limited human body, I read the transcripts and feel as though they are given in parables, just as when reading the words of Master Jesus. While reading, sometimes a window of light and understanding opens and I have an Aha! moment, while at other times I can read and be more curious than I ever was before.

There are times when we try to understand something with our human mind whereas the understanding should be rising from our hearts and from our spark of divinity. How can we understand an aspect of unity when we are drowned amidst duality and searching for a way to be rescued?

When you read some of these discourses which seem like parables, say a prayer and ask for the window of understanding from the heart to be opened to you. Say something like: *"In the name of the I AM THAT I AM, I ask that full understanding and wisdom be given to me now from these words. I ask that these words come to light and heal my body, my mind, my emotions, my spirit and my soul. I ask that I may grow from the wisdom derived from these words in every way possible."* In this way you enhance the results, and each new time that you read the same words you will benefit and receive what you need in that moment.

MANTRA FOR LIFE AND RESSURICTION
METATRON, CHANNELED NOVEMBER 29, 2002

Beloved of my own heart, I am Metatron. Take a deep breath with me. *Say over and over and over again:*
I am the life and the resurrection.
I am the resurrection and the life.

The two are one. It may seem like the two ends of the spectrum, but it is not a spectrum; it is a circle. So the ending is sitting right next to where the beginning is. I am the resurrection and the life; I am the life and the resurrection. "I am the resurrection and the life" will give you momentum for anything. You can say, *"I am the resurrection and the life"* of whatever was successful for you and you want to resurrect it. You can say, *"I am the resurrection and the life of my business."* You can say, *"I am the resurrection and the life of my abundance."* You can say, *"I am the resurrection and the life of my partnership."* And it is the most potent of the I AM Mantras. It is perhaps the crowning glory.

If you need your business to accomplish more, go to the momentum of "the life and the resurrection." If you need spiritual accomplishments, reflect in your mind and in your heart on the ultimate experience, and say over and over again, *"I am the resurrection and the life of my spiritual evolution; I am the life and the resurrection of my spiritual evolution."* If you want healing for your body or someone else's body, *"I am the resurrection and the life of this body; I am the life and the resurrection of this body."* If you want to take someone who is passing over from this world to the Light, create a tunnel of Light for them, weave the filament and Threads of Life and resurrection inside this tunnel and repeat, *"I am the resurrection and the life sending (name) to the Light; I am the life and the resurrection."*

I am the resurrection of that life. I am resurrection of that Light body. That one sentence is a complete sphere. It is the beginning and the ending. It is the Alpha and the Omega. It brings to life, and it takes that life to its completion and to its resurrection where it truly belongs. It is exactly the epitome of what is happening to your bodies and to your planet. This is the death of ignorance; this is the resurrection of remembrance.

This is why you have to move through chaos. You have no choice. Chaos will move through you whether you like it or not. Take this chaos, turn it into an alchemical substance; make gold out of this base metal. Let this work for you. This chaos is impregnated with peace. Burst the bubble, go inside, see the peace, become it. Then you will become the witness, and as the witness nothing can touch you; no one will even dare to attempt. You will be so powerful that you will be the epitome of the Almighty divine human.

Repeat any of the I AM mantras, any and all. Become one with the I AM, constantly say any of the I AM Mantras, even the simple ones are the most meaningful, like:
Light I AM. Love I AM. Bliss I AM.
I AM THAT I AM.
God I AM.

Be Still and Know that I AM God

Commentary: There are two important parts to this mantra. Coming to that place of stillness helps you harness the emotions which can run rampant and create havoc in your life. Have you ever meditated on the events of a situation after the fact only to realize that your emotions got the better of you and ran amuck leaving you embarrassed and others hurt? These are the times that you would feel fortunate to have the above mantra. Before you allow the rampant emotions to spew out and leave their marks everywhere, it will work wonders if you could remember to take a pause and say, "Be still and know that I AM God."

The second part of this mantra which is very potent and effective is the "know that I AM God" aspect. When you can still the mind, then you can go into that space of knowing that you are only the witness to God's actions, thoughts and decisions. Then you don't take things personally, because

God is the doer and not you. On the other hand, when you believe that God is the doer and the actions are God's, then you would think before you say or do things; what would God do in a situation like this? That pause to think before you act can itself bring stillness. It also can bring a chance to collect yourself and ask God for help. The question of what God would do in this situation can be followed by, *"In the name of the I AM THAT I AM, help me figure out what to do. Show me how you want it done."* This will then bring us back to that place of stillness to let God be the doer.

METATRON, CHANNELED NOVEMBER 29, 2002

Beloved of my own heart, I am Metatron. Take a deep breath with me.

Be still and know that I AM God

The more that you say the "Be still and know that I AM God", the greater the stillness that falls upon you. In that stillness, you can find oneness and union, peace and harmony. You will begin to have an understanding of the truth and a wisdom that is not found in any books. The more that you repeat this mantra, the easier it will be for you to look into the future and receive knowledge of events beforehand. This will prepare you to receive those events so that you are not taken by surprise. In this way you can process your thoughts and emotions before you are inundated with the surge of events or before your hasty actions have an adverse impact on others.

In oneness of the I AM, I am Metatron. So it is.

Triangle of Manifestation by Quan Yin

Commentary: This is an exercise to help bring specific objects or intentions into your life. It works best if you are very clear about what it is that you want (e.g., a red Mercedes, or a pet puppy). The more focused and clear that you are, the easier it will become to manifest through this exercise. When you have a very focused mental body, you are capable of manifesting whatever you desire. Your mind and your heart must both become involved in the exercise. You must will yourself from your mind and desire it from your heart.

In this exercise, Quan Yin uses the power of will in the solar plexus and the power of perceptual vision from the higher realms held in the third eye to bring the objects of your desires into manifest form. By using the solar plexus and third eye as the centers of focus, Quan Yin teaches us how we can bring the objects of our desire into our reality. As long as there is clarity about the object you want to manifest, you will have the ability to produce results quickly and easily. Sometimes the difficulty lies with lack of clarity or focus. If you are not clear, then take the time to decide upon exactly what you want. If you are not focused, then become determined to get focused. Discipline yourself to repeat the exercise until you have the object you want in your hand or in your life. This exercise works best with things or objects such as a new car, a new house, a pet, new clothes, new computer, etc.

It can also work with things like a new job, a new rose garden, a new swimming pool, a new office, a new set of bedroom furniture, a new house in the country, lighting fixtures in your living room, as long as you have figured out the exact details of the rose garden or office or bedroom furniture. Your ability to visualize the object is important in this exercise.

For issues and events that are more abstract or undecided, you can still use this exercise provided that you are willing to hold your focus on it until it gradually becomes clear. For example, a new relationship can be spun in this grid provided that you have very clear ideas about what you want in a relationship. A little bit of advance homework can bear wonderful results.

QUAN YIN, CHANNELED FEBRUARY 13, 2004

My child of Light, I am Quan Yin.

Create a triangle of Light — a triangle of blue white light — and spin that triangle. One point of the triangle sits in your third eye. You place your focus and intent upon manifesting the object of your desires. Another point is in your solar plexus. The third point would make an equilateral triangle outside of your body; if you drew two lines, one from your third eye and one from your solar plexus to meet at a point outside of your body, you would make an equilateral triangle. Then visualize placing the object of your desires in that point outside your body. Then begin by sending a beam from your third eye to that object and another beam from your solar plexus to that object. Lastly, send a beam of light that connects your third eye to your solar plexus. Then you begin to spin these three points around the triangle.

You may not know this process consciously. However, this is the alchemy used for manifestation in this realm of reality. The third eye is the opening to the higher realms and the Presence of your own I AM THAT I AM. It is the connection to the mind of God, while the solar plexus is the center for manifestation of the will of God. **Whatever you wish to manifest in this reality sits somewhere outside of your own body between these two points. Now to manifest it, you must make it a part of yourself.** To do this, create the triangle. Once you create the triangle, spin it. Spin the triangle by moving the energy from the third eye to the point outside, from the point outside to the solar plexus, from the solar plexus up to the third eye, and back to the outside again. This will energize the triangle while spinning. When energy moves from solar plexus to third eye, the object is sanctioned by the higher vibration of the third eye. It can now come from those realms into your reality. When the energy moves from the object into the solar plexus, the will of God is moving to the mind of God for the object to be manifested in this realm of reality.

This is the alchemy. You can manifest whatever you wish in this way. This technique is for the benefit of Light and for the highest wisdom. It is a manifestation technique to bring from the higher realms the object of desires to Earth. Those who are capable of manifesting the objects of their desires in alignment with Light, in service to Light, according to their mission of Light are allowed to use it.

Take a deep breath with me now. We will practice this exercise. Think of an object you wish to manifest. It can be a specific thing or a universal intention, an intention of service to all humankind or a simple object manifested quickly to prove to yourself that this technique really does work. Once you can see that intention clearly, place it in that point outside. Send a beam of light — blue-white light — from your third eye to the point outside of your body. Then send a beam of blue-white light from your solar plexus to the object. Finally send a beam of blue-white light from your third eye to your solar plexus and then begin to spin the entire triangle. (As the triangle spins, the object of desires moves into the solar plexus and then finds its way up to the third eye. It continues to move between the three points: into the solar plexus, up to the third eye, out to the third point and back into the solar plexus again.) Spin it faster and faster until the entire triangle becomes a bluish-white sphere of Light. It will then explode. At the point of explosion, it becomes one with you. And in that moment of oneness, you know that the object of that desire has been accomplished. It is brought from the higher realms to the realm of this reality for manifestation.

Continue to repeat the exercise daily as many times as you can remember to do it. A minimum of three times a day is a good start. The more frequently that you focus on practicing this exercise, the faster you can bring it into your reality. Do this every day until you have it in your hands or in your life. Do not stop until you have what you want. Be serious about what you want, and let the universe know how serious you are by repeating it. In this way, the universe can come to your assistance to bring results faster.

I am your mother, Quan Yin.

Awakening Visual Perception and Verbal Communication

Commentary: Metatron gave this healing meditation in response to someone requesting greater visual perceptions and understanding of the signs given by spirit. Sometimes we miss the signs given to us. At other times we misinterpret the signs. In extreme cases when we need or look for the signs, we feel as though we are blind or deaf to them. When we become anxious, we do not see or hear the guidance. Some people find that although they meditate and perform spiritual exercises, they do not have the personal experiences and can not see or hear the spiritual guidance from the Masters, the guides or their own Higher Self.

In the past, I have found myself in situations in which I did not notice the guidance or did not take it seriously enough; afterwards I was ready to kick myself. I too have requested that I might receive the signs more powerfully, or as Metatron puts it, more forcefully. The problem is that we actually get what we ask for. When we ask for it more forcefully, then that is what we get. For example, instead of getting the answer peacefully through a song or a piece of advice from a loving passerby, we hear it screamed in our face by an angry passerby, our pubescent teenagers or even our complacent pets who leave us smelly gifts around the house as reminders. Instead of seeing a deer or doe (which indicates gentleness) while crossing a suburban road, we may come across a skunk that brings the news of a stink-up! I have learned over the years to request so that if I do not get it right the first and second times with gentle nudges and hints, then kick me into gear (or worse!) the third time.

I now ask that the signs be given very clearly and definitively and perhaps just a little louder than the first and second times.

In the following meditation, Metatron is opening the visual chakra between the eyebrows for visual perception. For beginners, this exercise helps you to see more clearly and have visual perceptions which usually begin first by seeing lights of different colors and intensity. After a while, you may receive symbols which you then have to interpret. Such symbols usually come first thing in the morning while we are coming back from alpha state to wakeful consciousness or during meditation exercises as Metatron suggests. These symbols will have to then be interpreted by you based on your thoughts and the intentions that you may have put out to the universe. Vivid dreams are also windows for opening the perceptive inner eyes.

Metatron then moves to open the channeling chakra at the base of the neck — the center where we receive sound and verbal communication. This type of communication also usually begins with symbols; for example, the sounds of thunder and lightning before establishing contact. It feels as though God or the guides are announcing their presence through sounds. Verbal communication usually follows.

Remember to ask the name and lineage of the being who begins to communicate with or through you. It is common courtesy that the Master or guide who comes forth to speak with you would introduce themselves first and ask permission to speak or work with you. If you feel uneasy or unsure of the contact, say to the being, *"In the name of the I AM THAT I AM, I give you permission provided that you are of higher and brighter Light than I am."*

Remember that it does not serve you to work with a guide or Master who has less light than yourself. You will not be learning anything positive or valuable from such a presence, and you may contaminate your own energy field. Even your physical body can be detrimentally affected. People who use ouija boards or open themselves to channeling just any entity can open themselves to beings and entities who are lost — souls who have not found the Light or are stuck in the astral realms because of their low light or attachments to Earth. Some of these souls may even be good loving souls who have lost their lives suddenly and are as yet unaware that they are no longer in physical embodiment. Even if this were the case, I suggest that you avoid calling these entities to yourself or giving them permission to work with you until you are able to fully protect yourselves first and learn how to help them out of their misery. You will not serve anyone — neither them nor yourself — if you try to swim in these uncharted waters without the required expertise.

However, there are beneficial ways to request help for those in the astral realms. When you ask for relief on behalf of the souls in the astral realms, you are also helping to relieve Mother Earth of some of her burden. At this present time, prayers of this kind are greatly needed. Call upon the presence of Archangel Michael and his legions of Light and mercy, and ask for a vortex of Light to be opened up on behalf of the disembodied souls in the astral and suspended realms. A good prayer to use would be, *"In the name of the I AM THAT I AM, I call forth Archangel Michael and his legions of Mercy to open a portal or vortex of Light in this location, or one mile north of here, and to guide all souls to go through it to the Light. So it is. Amen."*

METATRON, CHANNELED OCTOBER 14, 2004

Beloved of my own heart, I am Metatron. Take a deep breath with me.

Focus your energy in the center of your third eye. Imagine as though you are looking with your eyes slightly rolled up and with both of your eyes looking to the point between your eyebrows on your forehead, the ajna center. Imagine a candle flame being placed in that center. The purpose of that candle flame is to reawaken the divine center for visual perception from the inner realms and to rekindle the light of the divine Self. This will reawaken your consciousness reconnecting you with the soul essence and to receive visual perception from the realms of the I AM THAT I AM.

Every day for a few minutes upon awakening and a few minutes at bedtime, focus your energies in crossing your eyes and looking at this center from inside. Visualize a candle flame burning, knowing that this flame is the flame of God Unity. And with the illumination of this flame, your visual perception and your connection to the higher realms will be established. Continue this practice for a consecutive period of nine days. And you will begin to have visual perceptions as you sit to meditate. These visual energies will begin by first seeing a profusion of lights — different colored lights. Sometimes lightning rods of white light, at other times, sparkles of different lights.

The more often you practice this exercise, the more quickly your visual perceptions will begin to occur. Once they begin, you must request the meaning behind each experience. The next phase of awakening occurs when you begin to also hear words spoken to you from the inner realms. The opening of that energy field is in the base of the neck, where your head is connected to your spine. For a while as this energy field is awakening, you may have pain in the base of your neck.

This is the opening of the energy field, the channeling chakras — the chakras where you receive verbal communication. Sometimes people open up this chakra before they open up the visual. In others, the perception is only visual, without commentary, without hearing any voices. It is important that both of these chakras be opened up. In this way, you will feel the guidance through visual perceptions and by hearing the verbal guidance. Inasmuch as you are looking at the world through your inner eye, the visual perception is not exactly the same as you have with your sensory means. But it is the knowing that comes with the inner vision. In the same way, hearing the spoken words is not like hearing someone speak to you directly, but it is the knowing. As time goes by, the sparks of knowing turn into words that are spoken to you from the inner realms, almost as though they are spoken in a hushed voice or communicated without being spoken.

In order to focus on opening the energy field at the back of your neck where the channeling charkas are located, it is also important that you become aware of that energy. The sensation would be as though a push or pressure is being placed in that area. The sensation is almost as though you need to have a neck adjustment, because your head is sitting slightly pushed on top of your neck, as though someone is pushing part of your head forward, and the pressure is painful. Also as you open up your third eye, you may feel headaches in the form of a band around your head exactly where the flame has been placed. But you have asked for these energies to be given to you. And it is a small price to pay for an important step in your spiritual growth.

Exercise every morning and every night to look at that point and see the flame illuminated. And focus on feeling the warmth of the flame. You may have an itchy or a tingling sensation in the space of the third eye. Also focus your energy in that space at the base of your neck, at the very point where the head sits over the neck, and feel the pressure that is pushing your head forward. That is when the energy is entering through that chakra and pushing the light into the opening. That may cause pressure which can feel as though your neck is sitting slightly crooked, and your head may feel pushed forward on your neck.

If it is your desire from now on that the guidance come to you more forcefully and that the window of opportunity will be more clearly defined to you, then it shall be done. But understand that when you ask for guidelines in this manner, then the results will come in this way.

With great love, I am your father, Metatron. So it is.

Temples and Retreats of the Ascended Masters

Commentary: The higher that we elevate ourselves in pursuit of spiritual growth, the greater our powers of manifestation will become. In this exercise, Metatron is teaching us to put our dream time to good use by asking to be taken to the Temples of Light and Wisdom every night during sleep. By receiving the teachings from the Masters, we will first awaken our subconscious mind to the higher truths. Gradually these truths will seep through to our normal everyday consciousness. Metatron teaches us to accelerate this process by journaling our dreams and by asking the Masters to help us recollect the memories from our dream time.

METATRON, CHANNELED APRIL 6, 2004

Beloved of my own heart, I am Metatron. Take a deep breath with me.

Every night as you go to bed, just before you fall asleep call upon the presence of Metatron (or any one of the Ascended Masters you feel a connection with), Archangel Michael, Lady Faith, and say: *"In the name of the I AM THAT I AM, I ask Metatron, Michael and Faith to take me to the highest temples and retreats of the Ascended Masters. While there, teach me and remind me of the highest truths that my body and being will benefit from. Help me to remember the truths that I learn and recollect in the Temples of Light during my wakeful consciousness."*

Then try to journal your dreams and your thoughts regarding those dreams. You may think you will remember them, but you will not. The process of writing them down is also in itself a healing and recollection. The realm of thoughts and dreams is an etheric realm. When you write the thoughts and dreams down on paper, you anchor the energy of that thought or dream into this reality. In fact, by writing you bring thoughts and dreams to the second dimension of reality. It is no longer in the third dimension; it moves further down to two dimensions. This can help to anchor the energy fully. This is why writing down your thoughts and journaling your dreams and ideas are great manifestation tools. You would be surprised how many ideas and thoughts can be processed into manifest form by focusing your attention on writing them down.

With all of my heart, with all of my love, I hold you dear to my own heart. I am your father, Metatron. So it is.

Part Four ~ Enlightenment

Introduction to Metatron and Enlightenment

The subject of enlightenment is much talked about and little understood. The premise is that the God Presence exists within every soul. When the soul recognizes and identifies with that God within, then the soul is ready for enlightenment. When the soul lives and breathes every moment of their life in that recognition, the soul becomes enlightened. This recognition helps the soul merge into the God Presence within so that me, my or mine no longer exists, and all is in oneness.

Someone once asked Sai Baba, an enlightened soul (Avatar) from India, "Are you God?" He answered, "You are God." Then he continued, "I have realized that fact and you haven't." That is really all there is to it.

Although mentally grasping this concept represents significant progress, there still remain additional steps to undergo. To reach the highest levels one must strive, abstain and work very hard. It is said that many lifetimes of austerity are necessary to reach enlightenment. Yet it is also believed that in the Age of Kali Yuga, simply remembering the name of God brings a soul to enlightenment. In contrast, in the Age of Sathya Yuga, the Age of Truth, souls live seven or eight hundred years, and spend their entire lifespan performing austerities before reaching enlightenment.

The difference is that in the Age of Sathya Yuga people live in peace, harmony and truth. It is a pleasure to be alive and a bonus to live a long life of austerities reaching to enlightenment. It seems like the icing on the cake. However, in the Age of Kali Yuga, where darkness and despair, untruth and corruption, chaos and confusion is prevalent, people have a difficult enough time remembering their own soul and the purpose of their soul's mission. Consequently, to remember the name of God amidst life's daily struggles is enough of an achievement to bring on enlightenment.

I am reminded of a story: A man died and went to the gates of Heaven where God and his angels were selecting the fate of the souls. He observed the procedure intently when a man came up for his judgment and his guardian angel read his life story. This man was a hardworking farmer. He rose early in the morning and thanked the Lord for all the blessings, had his breakfast, offered his day to the Lord and went to work until sunset. Then he returned to his home, washed himself and sat down to his meal, thanked the Lord for his blessings and went to bed. He did this for fifty years of his adult life. Then he died. God listened and said, "Send him to Heaven." The man was sent to Heaven.

The observing bystander became anxious and said, "This is not fair! This man did nothing but remember you two times a day, and you send him to Heaven. You are making it too easy!" God replied, "I will make it easy on you too if you do as I tell you." Then God asked the angels to bring an oil lamp. It was made of a round jar full of oil with a wick to light. God instructed the angel to light the wick, and said to the man, "Take this oil lamp and go back to Earth. Pay close attention night and day that the wick remains lighted continuously for seven days and that the oil does not spill from it. Whatever you do and wherever you go, this oil lamp must be with you. Do this for seven days.

The angels will be watching you and will keep the lamp full of oil at all times. If after the seven days you have accomplished this task, I will send you to Heaven too."

The man thought this to be an easy task. He decided to put all his efforts into it. He gave of himself, wholeheartedly determined to fully accomplish the task. The seven days and nights went by slowly but uneventfully. The man came back to the gates of Heaven with the lamp, accompanied by the guarding angel. The angel reported that the man had indeed succeeded in keeping the lamp lighted at all times, and no oil ever spilled out of the jar. God seemed very pleased and said to the man, "Please tell me, in this seven days and night of vigilance with the lamp, did you ever remember God's name or think of God at all?" The man said, "No, I was busy focusing on the lamp. All my attention went to keeping the wick lighted and the jar unspilled. I had no time to talk or think of anything else but the lamp." God listened intently and prompted the man expectantly, "You mean not even once did you think of God?" The man became annoyed and said, "You set me up with a difficult task; it was hard work. I was watching the lamp with every ounce of my being." God said, "Now do you see why I sent the hardworking farmer to Heaven for remembering my name twice a day?"

Such is our story in this age of chaos and confusion. We are juggling the many lamps in our lives trying to keep them lighted, and we are aiming at reaching enlightenment. In the process we become impatient with ourselves and others, we become angry and despondent (sometimes even angry at God and the Masters), and even disillusioned about the validity of it all. Throughout the process God is waiting patiently. The guarding angels and Masters are also beckoning us, praying for us, interceding on our behalf with God and intervening in our lives to remove obstacles, rectify problems and smooth out the path for our spiritual growth and ultimate goal of enlightenment.

The exercises in this section are meant to advance you toward that ultimate goal. The Master Metatron is the guiding force. As you will experience through the following pages, Metatron is one of the highest, brightest and greatest of God's archangels, much adored by God. He is also the driving force behind the entire creation. He is the guarding angel who has given us the teaching materials and the channeled messages, which are compiled in the form of the *Gifts* series. He acts as guide and master, offering his guidance and assistance to anyone who wishes to grow and to mature on the path of enlightenment. As an Ascended Master he has experienced the trials and tribulations of physical embodiment, and he knows the difficulties of entrapment in physical matter. He has great compassion, although at times he admits he has to be cruel in order to be kind. But even that is for our own benefit and to further our growth and maturity on the path of Light.

To further your experience as you read this section, call upon Metatron in his aspects as Archangel Metatron, as lesser YWHW (Yahweh), as El Shaddai and as Enoch the prophet. Ask for his blessings, his guidance and his presence for your soul growth from this moment on. Pause here (or at the end of this introduction) for a moment and call upon Metatron in your own words, with your own heartfelt desires, and feel his blessings.

Metatron is considered *"The greatest of Angels, second only to God"* and a *"lesser Yahweh"* in stature and power, which God bestows upon him before his entire Heavenly court, proclaiming *"My name is in him."* (Guiley, pp. 240-1). Huge in size, he stands on top of the Tree of Life as the Angel of YHWH and is in charge of the House of Ketter which corresponds to the crown chakra on the human body. Archangel Sandalphon, another aspect of Metatron, holds the tenth position at the root chakra — The numbers begin at ten and go up to one at the top.

Some scholars believe that the name itself, as well as the bearer of the name, was supposed to be a secret only to be revealed to those who have access to altered states of consciousness where the name and the energy would be revealed to them. *Zohar*, the book of splendor, is a compilation of mystic teachings of the Kabbalah. It equates the name Metatron with Shaddai, one of the names of God. The mystical numerology called Gematria, assigns sacred numbers to the letters of the alphabet. Both Metatron and Shaddai have numerical values of 314, which connects them mystically.

"Metatron is sometimes called the shining light of the Shekinah" (Zargar, p. 241). Shekinah is the Hebrew name for the Holy Spirit. He is also described as *"he whose name is like that of his Master"* (Ibid, p. 241). Great names, qualities and functions have been attributed to Metatron. There is no splendor, beauty, brilliance, brightness, greatness, wisdom or power that God withholds from him. Another of Metatron's many names is Sasnigiel, who is considered to

be "the prince of the world," one of the Angel (Princes) of the presence, and a seraphim. Sasnigiel is one who bows down to Zazriel according to *3 Enoch*.

Elsewhere in the chart as one of the names of Metatron, Zazriel itself is mentioned. "Angels of Presence" or "Prince of Countenance" are the high level angels who can withstand being in the presence of the Throne of God and look at God's face. Metatron is such an angel. Others named as such are Sandalphon, Zagagael, Jehoel, Sabaoth and Yefefiah. *The Encyclopedia of Angels* lists all the above names together with over 90 more as numerous alternative names of Metatron.

Other names of Metatron are Prince of Wisdom, Yoho-El-Yah, El Shaddai or Shaddai. El Shaddai is known to be a powerful force to call upon, especially for repelling demons. He is also known as the Angel of Protection. El Shaddai was so powerful that in the Middle Ages, the name was used in amulets for protection and placed above the doorways of houses and shops to protect the owners and visitors from harm, to prevent premature death and to repel demons. It also serves to remind all of the power of God. Jews and Gentiles both used the name El Shaddai in these amulets known as the Mezuzot (plural). A mezuzah (singular) was an amulet made of parchment scrolls inscribed with prayers and with the names of God and angels.

Strict instructions were to be followed for its crafting, such as, "It is to be written only on Monday, in the fifth hour, over which the sun and the Angel Raphael preside, or on Thursday, in the fourth hour, presided over by Venus and the angel Anael." (Guiley, p.242). A small wooden case would be built to hold the mezuzah inside. A small window was cut into the box such that the name El Shaddai could show through it from the parchment scroll.

People carried small mezuzot for protection as personal amulets. Other angels inscribed inside the parchment were Michael (angel of protection), Gabriel (messenger of God), Azriel (angel of death), Raphael (angel of healing), Uriel (guardian of inner light), Anael (angel of sexuality and creativity), Zadkiel (angel of disciplines, order and transmutation), Yofiel (or Jofiel the angel of wisdom, prince of Torah, in the Old Testament. Yofiel is also another name for Metatron.)

Bible verses and other names of God were added with prayers to the Mezuzah. These amulets are still in use today, as Metatron in his varied capacities continues to work with Earth and humankind. The nature of his work is still the same. However through channeled materials New Age literature is becoming more familiar with Metatron. As a result we are beginning to have a more personal and loving relationship with those aspects of Metatron which have had Earthly lives in physical embodiment.

As always, it is much easier to understand and grasp the nature of a being from our human standpoint if we can identify with them on the same level. Working with those aspects of Metatron as an Ascended Master who has had human embodiments and feels the struggles and pain of human physicality makes the experience all the more real. The enormity of Metatron's task as the creator of the entire manifest creation, which includes the whole universe and more, is somewhat beyond our human grasp. It makes the experience somewhat unreal as the gap between us seems so vast. It is practically an unimaginable concept to define where we end as humanity and where she/he begins as the creative force, and how ultimately we all return to Metatron's beingness to reach back to the oneness of God Unity.

In order to begin absorbing all of this, it helps to study Metatron's incarnations on Earth with human experiences and a past history. Enoch was such a being. Rosemary Ellen Guilley in *The Encyclopedia of Angels*, tells the story of Enoch as such:

> *"Enoch, the son of Jared and seventh descendant of Adam and Eve, is taken to Heaven by angels, for God has chosen him to be a scribe and a witness to the consequences of sin and the rewards of righteousness. He is taken to different levels of Heaven and hell, learns the mysteries of the cosmos and the celestial realms, sees the future, including the flood, the end of the world and the last judgment. He is given a Heavenly body of light and shown the books of knowledge. Enoch is sent back to Earth in order to pass on the teachings to his sons and others. God then takes Enoch back into Heaven. In some accounts God transformed him into Metatron, giving him 365,000 eyes and 36 pairs of wings. One of his functions as Metatron is to be the scribe of Heaven" (p. 115).*

Enoch's genealogy is given in the Book of Genesis 4:1-24 and 5:1-32, starting with Adam and Eve and progressing all the way to Noah. Enoch was the seventh descendant from Adam and Eve, and Noah was three generations from Enoch. According to Genesis, Jared, Enoch's father was

165 years old when he had Enoch and lived to be 962 years old. Enoch became the father to Methuselah when he was 65 years old. The Book of Genesis states that

"Enoch walked with God after the Birth of Methuselah three hundred years, and had other sons and daughters. Thus all the days of Enoch were three hundred and sixty-five years. Enoch walked with God; and he was not, for God took him." (Genesis 5:21-24).

The general understanding is that Enoch recorded and passed on the information that God desired him to bring to Earth, and he was then taken up or "translated" into Heaven where he became a fiery angel with 72 wings, possibly an aspect of Archangel Metatron.

The recorded information seems to have passed on and been preserved even through the great flood. Some scholars believe that Noah took it upon himself to preserve the manuscripts or that he reproduced them by divine inspiration from the Holy Spirit. What remains of the *"Enochian Manuscripts"* is divided into three categories known as *1 Enoch*, *2 Enoch* and *3 Enoch*.

1 Enoch is the oldest of the three and dates back to two centuries before Christ. It may have been written both in Hebrew and Aramaic. It was known by Jews, Christians and the Essene alike and is believed to have influenced the language and nature of the New Testament of the Bible. It has 107 chapters and is divided into five books. It is called the *Ethiopic Book of Enoch* (Guiley, p. 115). The first book is about the fall of the "Watchers." (see Archangel Michael's Protection section). Enoch's role in the story is this: Enoch witnessed in a dream vision the pleas of humanity to be rescued from the corruption that had become rampant after the fall of the Watchers and from the demands of the Nephilim children. He also witnessed instructions issued to the four Archangels of God to destroy these dark angels, and Enoch informed their leader. The leader asked Enoch's intercession which he brought before the Throne of God, but to no avail. Enoch is taken to the Throne of God and is received by a dazzling bright shining being (God), who explains to Enoch why punishment is necessary and is shown the *"Foundation of Earth and the Firmament of Heaven"* (Guiley, p. 115).

The names of the holy Archangels of Light are given to him as Uriel (Suruel), Raphael, Michael, Gabriel, Rajuel and Saragael (another name of Metatron). These are the ones that are to be involved in bringing justice, healing, protection, light and righteousness back to Earth. Enoch sees in Earth's future the cleansing through the great flood and the survival of the righteous led by Noah, a righteous man and Enoch's own descendant. When Noah was born, his father Lamech (who was the grandson of Enoch) complains that the infant looks like an angel, and Enoch consoles him by telling him that through Noah the righteous shall be rescued and will be seated in Heaven on the Throne of Honor (Guiley, p.116).

2 Enoch is called the *Slavonic Enoch*. A text with mysterious origins, the only available originals are in Slavonic language. Most Slavonic literature dates from the Middle Ages, and yet it is suspected that this book was written around the first century. However, no originals exist in any other language. *2 Enoch* is about events in Enoch's life up to the time of the flood and the birth of Melchizedek, the supernatural son of Nir, who is brother to Noah. Melchizedek was born to Nir and his wife Sophanim, both very elderly.

When Nir found out that Sopanim was pregnant while sterile and without any sexual relations, he sent her away in shame. She died, and Nir asked Noah to help bury her to hide the scandal. They wrapped her body in a black garment and went away to dig a grave in secret. Upon their return they found that a child had been born from the dead body, the size and stature of a three-year-old and wearing the badge of priesthood on his chest. The babe spoke and blessed the Lord. Although terrified, Noah and Nir realized that the glorious priesthood had been renewed in this child and returned to their blood line.

I have included the description of the birth of Melchizedek as a descendant of Enoch here because it portrays another important and interesting observation. In my first *Gifts* book, I have stated that Metatron is a great archangelic force and that Melchizedek is our Universal Logos, the Word or God for our entire universe. These two descriptions paint a grand picture of cosmic beings highly evolved beyond our grasp. Yet here in *Gifts II,* we are dealing with the human aspects of cosmic beings in the form of Enoch — a strong and powerful prophet of God — and Melchizedek his great-great grandson, a supernatural child born through immaculate conception into a three year old body. Here we see both of those cosmic beings from a human perspective. Metatron coming to Earth as Enoch and Melchizedek returning the glorious and righteous priesthood to Earth.

Both beings are known and accepted in the New Age literature as Ascended Masters and as great beings of Light who have offered their Light in service to humankind. In their capacity as great cosmic beings we can revere and honor them, and we know that their guidance comes to us from the highest source. Yet, it is in their capacity as physically embodied human beings that we can fully identify with them. These are mortals who conquered the duality and darkness of the mundane levels of existence and transcended the physical body to translate to Light. They then became the Ascended Masters, our own beloved older brothers whom we cherish, love and obey through their channeled guidance and messages.

3 Enoch, also called the *Hebrew Apocalypse*, dates to the 5th or 6th century and is an account of a journey to the high Heavens, including the highest Heaven where the Throne of God is located. In this story, Rabbi Ishmael (who was a well known and respected Palestinian scholar) goes up to Heaven in a vision because God desires for him to see the high Heavens. There he is greeted by Seraphim, Cherubim and Ophanim who are the highest angels of the high Heavens. They gaze at him with disregard through their dazzlingly brilliant eyes. The fire and the light from their eyes is too bright for the rabbi, and he withdraws from them. But God reprimands these angels and instructs them to lower their eyes to relieve the rabbi. God instructs Metatron to guide the rabbi through the various parts of Heaven. During the tour of Heaven, Metatron tells the rabbi his own story of coming to Earth and taking a physical embodiment as Enoch.

Rabbi Ishmael is believed to have died in 132 CE, placing the timeframe of his life on Earth long enough after Enoch's so that Enoch could conceivably have taken another embodiment and incarnated back on Earth as Ishmael. In one of the main sections of *3 Enoch*, the rabbi is told that he himself was Enoch, and the story of Enoch's translation from his physical embodiment to his ascended state in the

Heavens is described. On one hand, it is possible that the rabbi's name has been used by the authors of *3 Enoch* to add authenticity since the book was written several centuries after Enoch's lifetime. Yet on the other hand, elaborate and other-worldly details do appear in the descriptions.

The account relates Ishmael's ascension to the various layers of Heaven to participate in the ceremony of the Recitation of Qedussah (sanctus or sacred devotional hymns). It also gives an elaborate description of the angelic hierarchies, the various courts of Heavenly law and the tour of Heaven. (Guiley, p. 118). In the Heavenly court, Ishmael is shown that there are great angelic princes known as YHWH (Yahweh). There are 72 of these princes who rule various kingdoms of the world. The prince of the world is the head of this hierarchy and the advocate for the world. When the court convenes, God sits on the Throne with the Angel of Mercy to the left, Angel of Justice to the right and Angel of Truth in the front, directly facing God. The Angel Scribes stand above and below the throne, and Angels of Destruction stand in front of God, ready to carry out instructions. The Ophanim and the Seraphim Angels surround the Throne with tongues like torches of fire and walls of lightning. Clouds of flame and fire surround all, and underneath them are the gigantic holy creatures that hold the Throne. Fire flows from a river beneath everything.

Metatron reveals to Ishmael the secret of creation by showing him the cosmic fiery letters with which the entire creation came to manifest form. These may have been the sacred geometric shapes known as plutonic solids, of which I have written in *Gifts III*. On the other hand, this may be the original concept of "the Word" mentioned in the book of Genesis, "In the beginning was the Word and the Word was with God and the Word was God." Metatron also explains the divine power behind the sacred names and the importance and benefits of the repetition of the divine name (Guiley, p. 119). *3 Enoch* reveals the entire history of Earth and its final phase or ending, which is in stark contrast to the doom and gloom prophecies rampant today. The end time prophecies of *3 Enoch* speak of the return of the Messianic kingdom to Earth. The tale of the Messianic kingdom is inscribed on the Paragod, the veil that surrounds the Throne of God and holds the brilliance of God within it. The Messianic kingdom relates to the return of the Messiah to Earth and to the coming forth of 1000 years of peace to Earth. The return of purity and innocence will promote peace and harmony on Earth. The Messiah, expected by many religions, returns with many of his righteous disciples (who have also become Ascended Masters) to walk on Earth and to free Earth and humankind as well as all other souls from the darkness and misery of forgetfulness of their own divine origin as a spark of Light from the heart of God.

My *Gifts III* book in particular focuses on the return of the Messiah, his origin, his gifts for Earth and his mission, including the history of the 1000 years of peace and return of the Messianic kingdom. The advent of the return of this kingdom, according to the channeling from Metatron, is the year 2005. Spring Equinox of 2005 (March 20-21) denotes the entry point to the 1000 years of peace on Earth. August 12th of the same year is set for mass awakening of the souls to their divine spark of oneness and for reaching critical mass. Within one year from that date, Metatron and the Ascended Masters plan to bring multitudes of human souls to the awakened state.

This means that the entire population of Earth has the opportunity to awaken to their divine mission and to begin to tip the scale in favor of the Light. Choosing service to Light in a spiritually awakened state will help us move toward peace and harmony. We will move from a life of survival and self-preservation — where our personalities and our egos are in charge — to a life of service and living in love, serving to preserve our offspring and our planet Earth as one community and one world. This state is expected imminently by Metatron and the Masters.

Meanwhile, the cleansing effect of all the above is coming to the surface. As we let go of darkness and negative emotions, they come to the surface to be released. Their coming to the surface is felt as greater frenzies of emotional and mental energies. And the cleansing effects come in the form of earthquakes, tsunamis and hurricanes, which we have already witnessed. The global warming and the melting of the icebergs at both poles are all Mother Earth's way of cleansing herself from the pollution that has become rampant on her physical body.

Behind the cleansing awaits the return of the Messianic kingdom, the arrival of which has been prophesied to be the year 2012. The Mayan prophecies call 2012 "Entry into No Time." This means that time as we know it in this cycle of events will come to its conclusion and a new cycle will begin. Metatron has given, through channeling, a seven-year cycle which precedes the entry into the new age of Light. That cycle will begin in the year 2005, and stretch over the seven years leading to 2012.

In this seven year cycle, we will be building the fabric of light over our globe with the help of the Masters of Light and the Angelic Forces of Light. We will also be increasing the quotient of light within our own individual hearts and beingness to reach greater levels of spiritual evolution and wisdom. Many healing modalities, clearing and protection techniques, prayers, invocations, decrees and mantras are becoming available to humanity for the purpose of achieving these ends. The New Age resource materials, including those presented through this series, and teachings of the Ascended and living Masters are more readily available to humankind. The wisdom and knowledge which was withdrawn from humankind in the past due to misuse and abuse is now brought to humanity by the grace and efforts of the Ascended Masters and the Angelic Forces of Light.

Christ Maitreya, the World Teacher, and Sanat Kumara, our Planetary Logos, are making their presence available here on Earth and are offering their guidance and assistance to humankind. Christ Maitreya is here to prepare all souls to receive their first and second initiations on the path of Light for greater spiritual evolution. He is also preparing the more highly evolved souls to receive their third and fourth initiations from Sanat Kumara. These souls are preparing for their levels of Mastery. The future of our world depends on the evolution of these souls to the Mastery levels in service to Ascended Masters of Light.

These are our future leaders and decision makers — those trained by the Masters of Light to take charge of running our world according to universal and cosmic laws of divine origin. They will put our planet on the map of the galaxy and universe as a civilized and enlightened world capable of holding its own and making a difference, not just from a global perspective but on interplanetary and galactic levels of interaction and communication. During the zenith of the Atlantean times, the Earth was the hub of intergalactic congregations. Over the ensuing few thousand years — following the fall of Atlantis and the emersion of the planet into lower vibration — Earth has lost its attraction as a hub for the congregation of highly evolved beings from around the galaxy.

In *Gifts III*, I have gone into greater depth describing various levels of spiritual evolution and the importance of the return of Christ Maitreya and Sanat Kumara to Earth. The main theme in *Gifts III* is the significance of the return of the World Teacher, or Planetary Christ, and the Planetary Logos as well as their teachings, healing techniques and meditational journeys designed to raise our own vibration of light through their energies. The purpose of *Gifts III*, according to instructions from Christ Maitreya and Sanat Kumara, is to help those who seek higher spiritual evolution to attain it through connection with these Masters through reading the book and taking the meditational journeys. Metatron and other Ascended Masters have been greatly involved in preparing the grounds for the coming forth of Christ Maitreya and Sanat Kumara. This is a project that has been millions of years in the making.

Those of us in physical embodiment during this present time of Earth's evolution are fortunate to see these efforts bear fruit. Yet the price we pay for our participation is that as pioneers we are mapping the unknown, and there are no guidelines or how-to manuals available to us. Where we are going no one has gone before, and the fact that our teachers are not in physical embodiment does not make our job

191

any easier! There are no normal classroom settings where we can learn the "tricks of the trade" or find the tools or gears to prepare us for the ride. It does not help that we hold a very small minority of people. According to Metatron, the New Age spiritual movement has had a membership of less than one-tenth of one percent of the population of Earth up until August 12th of 2005. Since then, that number has potentially increased to a full one percent, 0.9 of whom are novices who have only just joined us.

Therefore, do not be anxious if for a month or two before another cleansing cycle like an earthquake, hurricane, man-made disaster, an attack or a war you feel out of sorts, experience headaches, stomach upset or muscular pain for which the medical community can find no answers or explanation. The reason is your sensitivity to the changes of weather patterns. It is the release of the pain of Earth that you feel in your muscles, bones and inside your head. This translates to pains, aches and lack of ability to function normally when no external causes can be found. The external reason is not you but the world around you of which you are but a reflection. After all, as Metatron has said, the microcosm (us) is only the reflection of the macrocosm (our world). And as the mystical saying goes: "As above so below; as within so without."

As Ken Wilber states in his book *Up From Eden*:
"We must go whole-bodily to God, failing that, we fall into dissociation, repression, inner fragmentation, ultimate transcendence is thus not ultimate annihilation of the levels of creation, but rather their ultimate inclusion in spirit. The final transcendence is the final embrace. To return to the sources it is not necessary to destroy and annihilate the lower levels. It is necessary

only to transcend them, to cease identifying exclusively with them...we take all the lower levels with us out of love and compassion, so that all levels eventually are reconnected to the source." (Raynolds, p. 119).

Our objective in reaching enlightenment is to spiritize the lower levels so that they too become divine. After all, Metatron has been telling us for as long as I have been listening to him that the purpose of coming to these lower levels of dense matter is to spiritize them and bring them to Light. Once done, no one will ever be lost again, lost in the darkness of ignorance and pain or in the struggles of mental, emotional and physical turmoil.

Furthermore, Metatron reminds us that spiritizing matter alone will not cut the mustard any longer. We must also begin to materialize spirit. When we begin to blow the breath of spirit into the body of matter and ascertain that it does indeed infuse the physical body of matter, then and only then is the work complete, can we all then call it a day and get ready to go home. How many sages and saints, Buddhas and bodhisattvas have we encountered who have gone through their own struggles, borne the fruits of their austerities by reaching levels of Mastery and their own final enlightenment, only to realize that the world of matter is still immersed in its misery, pain and darkness? Matter until spiritized will call upon the compassionate sage, Master, Avatar, Buddha or Bodhisattva and will demand their return to Earth until all matter has been spiritized. A phrase that Metatron has coined in our channeling, the spiritization of matter refers to the return to glorious brilliance of its own divine light, in oneness with the Source in God Unity.

As Ken Wilber put it so aptly:

"Thus at ultimate enlightenment or return to spirit, the created world can still exist, it just no longer obscures spirit, but serves it. All the levels remain as expressions of Atman (true Self), not substitutes for Atman...all the lower levels are allowed to participate in absolute enlightenment and bathe in the glory of spirit. The mineral, as mineral, the plant, as plant, and the animal, as animal, could never be enlightened — but the bodhisattva takes all manifestation with him to paradise, and the bodhisattva vow is never to accept enlightenment until all things participate in spirit. There is, to my mind, no nobler conception than that." (Ibid).

The exercises that follow are meant to help you absorb such noble concepts, embody the spirit of that nobility and become illuminated with the Light of God Unity, or **ENLIGHTENED!**

Eternal Union: Citron and Peach-Pink, Male and Female Rays of the Seventh Golden Age

Commentary: Metatron gives this discourse in the company of many Masters of Light. This message was received on November 30, 2000 and is the oldest discourse in this book. It is important to remember, however, that some of the discourses are landmark events which effect our entire life span and beyond. This is one such event. It is relevant and effective regardless of when you read the information. He speaks of the ending of the age of karma, or the age of cause and effect, and entering into the Age of Bliss. He gives us the energies of the masculine and the feminine Rays which bring forth the vibration of the male and female for the new age we have entered. Every Ray emanates a certain color which vibrates through the environment as sound. Therefore, the color of each Ray sets the pace for the vibration of the energy of the time or the age. Color has a sound and sound has colors attached to it. This is obvious in higher dimensions, and it becomes a noticeable quality as individuals grow in their awareness beyond the five senses.

We can enter into the energies of the new age if we tune into the vibration of it. The vibration has a color, and through the color, a sound. Metatron is giving us the tools to enter into the portals of light and to bring forth the golden age through these energies. He teaches us to open the portals of energy, move through the void (which is the death of ego), find the light, merge with it and bring back to this reality the essence of what we have found: Eternal Union. The male and female of the Seventh Golden Age unite in oneness inside the portal of light. The benefit of this exercise in our daily life is to reach to that space of Eternal Union in our mundane reality. When we can find oneness in this three-dimensional realm, then we can permanently establish Heaven on Earth.

This discourse was given to members of our New Jersey group. The leader of this group is my dear friend and cohort Lucille Kluekas. Lucille and her group mentioned in the acknowledgements have been actively working together with Masters of Light in anchoring energies, opening new energy portals and consistently working in service to the light for two decades. I joined them over a decade ago. The Masters take great pleasure in sending me to New Jersey at times of important landmark events to work with Lucille and her group.

In this discourse, Metatron says, "All things begin with you and they end with you." This is another example of truth where the devotion and dedication of a few benefits the multitudes and masses. The energies that were given in this discourse were anchored through a three-day cycle in which we worked with the Masters to accomplish the anchoring of the energies of Eternal Union. As you read this discourse, you will receive the energies through your own body and magnify its impact through your conscious participation in the process.

METATRON, CHANNELED NOVEMBER 30, 2000

Beloveds of my own heart, I am Metatron.

In the company of Archangel Michael, our Lord Melchizedek the Universal Logos, The Presence of the I AM, the essence of The Undifferentiated Source, in the company of Goddess Pele, Goddess Hecate, Goddess Quan Yin, Goddess Hathor, the Beings of Light from Orion, the Beings of Light from Sirius, the Beings of Light from the Pleiades, the Beings of Light from Arcturus, and the Beings of Light from the Milky Way, your own home, I open this day of celebration, this day of jubilation.

All things begin with you and they end with you. How much do you believe in this? Perhaps not enough. I say this one more time, hoping that it will run shivers through your body so that you can connect with me and the essence of the truth that I speak: **things begin with you and they end with you.**

This is the beginning of a new era. Exactly one year ago (November 1999) we opened new portals of energy. We anchored energies to hold the Earth stable such that the shifts as they were predicted to happen would no longer be necessary to happen. This we did together — all of you and all of us — the Masters of Light. That was the ending of the phase of disasters. You may still see some destruction around you, but its nature and the gravity is insignificant in comparison to what could have or would have happened. (Earthquakes, floods, hurricanes and tsunamis are happening much more frequently since the turn of the century.)

Now let me tell you about the beginning. We have lived together through the age of karma, or cause and effect. This relates to when you create a reality, or you cause something to come into your reality, and its effect follows you until that cycle is over. Well, that cycle is over!

When that cycle ended, we moved from the Universal Law of Cause and Effect to the Universal Law of Divine Love. We have worked with Universal love, and we have anchored together the beginning of it. The Universal Law of Divine Love was anchored with help from Quan Yin. (November 1999 marks that event.)

BLISS AND ETERNAL UNION

Now, let me tell you about the beginning. One day in a gathering, I asked, "What is beyond love?" And everyone asked me back, "What *is* beyond love?" And I said, "BLISS."

Together we have begun to prepare for the Age of Bliss. Through the pains which all of you have endured to anchor The Bliss on Earth, you have become the pillars of light.

With all your prayers of love and all the light that you have sprinkled around the world, you have brought forth the Age of Bliss. I begin again by asking you, what is beyond Divine Love? What is beyond Bliss?

The answer is: **Eternal Union and Rapture.** At the beginning of this phase, I bring you these new energies, the energies of Eternal Union and Rapture. For the next three days try to be mindful of receiving these energies and plan to have no agenda until this phase is complete. Then we will see how far your bodies are willing to yield to and absorb the energies that are coming forth. We will then recalibrate you according to your individual needs. (This will be done by your intention. As you read these pages, if you wish to receive the recalibration, say, *"I ask Metatron to recalibrate me according to my individual needs."*)

I would like you to envision the male essence and the female essence of this new energy. The energy of Eternal Union and the energy of Rapture is spoken of sporadically in the scriptures or in historical accounts of the lives of saintly people. I bring you the essence of this sacred quality in a color. This color is now becoming very fashionable. It is called citron. It is a very pale yellowish-green color *(the color of the young inner leaves of a romaine lettuce).* That is the masculine aspect of this new ray, the essence of which you are about to anchor into the grid of the Earth. The feminine aspect is a combination of peach and pink, very light peachy-pink. The two combined hold the balance for the energy of Eternal Union. The next Universal Law — the Rapture of Union — will take you beyond that of karma, beyond that of love, beyond that of bliss and into the ultimate point of union where duality is no more. The Rapture of Union, or Eternal Union, is all there is. Oneness is all there is.

Why is it important that we bring forth this energy? Because this is the vibration of the true home for the new Ascended Earth. Is it true that Earth would have to vibrate a different frequency in order to be considered a star and become ascended? Yes, it is true. For that to happen, vibration is necessary. Sound and vibration are one. Sound vibrates colors. Colors can take you to the same source as sound can. If you combine sound and color together, the vibration can teleport you from any point to any point. Where we are about to go has not come into the realm of existence as yet. It is non-form. It is pure matter. It is pure energy. Furthermore, it is vibration in its stillness. In order to vibrate harmoniously with the stillness of the universe and gradually become one with that stillness yet remaining in physical matter, you need to wrap yourself in these two vibrations of color and sound — the citron and the peach pink.

As I open this portal of energy for you, envision that your merkaba fields (bodies of light around your own body) are activated. For the activation process, fill your merkaba with the citron and the pale pink-peach colors. Envision you are inside a pink-peach bubble of light. The combination of these two colors in the form of streaks begins to fill your merkaba field. You feel the vibration in your heart and in your head. Envision expanding your merkaba field, and unite it with the pulse from the universe in accordance with the heartbeat of the central core of the universe.

THE HEARTBEAT OF THE UNIVERSE

The next level is that in which your heartbeat is united with the heartbeat of the universe, the Omniverse and beyond into the cosmos. Then beyond the cosmos, all as one, with what I have called the Omnivos or Cosmivos. In this level the multidimensional cosmos come together, and the heartcore of that essence brings you to the heart of The Undifferentiated Source. It is beyond your imagination and comprehension. And yet I am asking you to do the impossible by imagining, envisioning, accepting, believing and trusting that it exists and that it has to come into form. That which has never before materialized is now coming into form.

For the first three days after this exercise, you may feel achy and you may need extra sleep. This is because of the anchoring of these new vibrations in your body. Accept all of this as natural. You are becoming the Light of the Adam Kadmon body seed. (Adam Kadmon is the body made of pure light which God had intended for humankind according to the original plan. That was before we moved into the great density of the three dimensional realm and became solid bodies of dense matter.) The seed of light was never meant to hold this much density and yet this much light all at once. This is the true nature of the duality in which you live.

MEDITATION JOURNEY TO ENTER THE PORTAL OF LIGHT

Take a deep breath and let me take you through the portal of light. Inhale deeply. With the exhale become aware of a pulsation. Go into the wave pattern of the pulse of the universe. You enter into a portal that is in a shape of a diamond. To go through the portal you need to focus on the colors. It is the colors that will take you beyond form. It is the citron and the peachy-pink. You may see a pearlescent color. Let it pull you into the portal of energy. As you move through, you may feel a sensation in the space of your heart chakra in the center of your chest. This is what the Kabbalist (one who knows the secrets of the Kabbalah, a Jewish mystery school) calls DA-AT...death. This is the void through which you have to enter and out of which you achieve Eternal Union.

Enter the portal. Reach the void. Allow the void to engulf you. Know that when you enter the unknown, you will merge with the essence of Pure White Light. Upon your entry into Pure White Light a Great Being is waiting for you. This Great Being may take the form of a Master that you already know. The essence, however, is beyond what you have as yet experienced in this body. This Great Being will have the power to pull you through the void and back out again. Once you accomplish this mission, you will be walking on a path of greater service to the Light. You will be instrumental in bringing forth the energies of Eternal Union to Earth, entry into the Golden Age of The Oneness of All Beings, the Great Age of God Unity. Pause and take a deep breath. Think of what you would like to wish for. Ask the Great Being for a gift and offer yourself in service to the Light.

My prayer is that mundane life would become easy and harmonious for you. You need peace and harmony as well as abundance and prosperity in your lives. To receive your vocation of service from the Great Being, please first ask that your mundane level needs and desires be met, including comfort, luxury, peace, joy in your heart and mind. Then ask to follow the path of service and the new vocation that is offered to you. Ask for the achievement of all your goals in pure Joy and Rapture. This is the new paradigm which will bring forth Eternal Union.

Pause and take a deep breath, and ask for whatever else you desire. If you wish for a partner to experience the essence of that Eternal Union, ask for such a partner. Those of you who have an existing partner, ask that you and your existing partner receive the comforts of life and peace of mind so that the eternal flame, or the twin flame, is fully ignited in both your hearts.

Move with the colors through the sound barriers. Break the sound barriers. Move through the void. Let the void move through you. Have no fear. To attain Rapture, you have to move through the void. The Great Being is waiting for you and guiding you to the final goal. Take your time. Enjoy.

Ask this Great Being to give you a sign or a name by which you might know these energies and feel their presence. Pause, take a deep breath and listen for sounds, for a name, a sign, a symbol or a feeling of energy. Pause and communicate with the being. Take as much time as you need. Feel the energies. If you are unable to receive a name or a symbol, then say, *"In the name of the I AM THAT I AM, I ask to receive all that is in my highest wisdom and light according to my divine purpose.*

The time has come to return. Remember that this portal of energy, this dimensional realm, this crack in time and space is open and available to you to visit again. Remember that the secret code for entry is to follow the sounds and the colors.

As the diamond shaped portal opens before you, the sounds and the colors will pull you through the center of the portal and will bring you back to this reality. It is as simple as this.

To experience this again when you wish to go on this journey, begin to pulse from your heart in rhythm with the heart of the universe. And in this way, with every pulse from your heartcore, send back the pulse of love through the universe all the way to the heartcore of The Undifferentiated Source (which is God in the highest essence without form). The Great Being will continue to activate, decode, download and recalibrate all the necessary information and data into your body according to the will of your I AM presence. This process will continue from this moment until the new recalibration automatically takes you to the next level (at the end of three days).

We are now complete and the energy is anchored. The grid is vibrating through the Earth and reintegrating all the necessary energies to enter into the Seventh Golden Age and the energies of Eternal Union. Together in this new phase, we witness great life unfolding in Earth's history. In your love, I stand at your feet in the presence of all the beings of Light from all the constellations and all the beings that hold you dear in their hearts. In the loving presence of the Undifferentiated Source, in the loving ever-present (Ehyeh Asher Ehyeh) I AM THAT I AM.

I am your humble servant, Metatron. So it is.

SUMMARY OF STEPS FOR ENTRY INTO THE PORTAL OF ETERNAL UNION
1. Call upon Archangel Michael, Metatron, Melchizedek

and the Great Being of Light who holds the energies of Eternal Union.

2. Envision a portal of light opening with pearlescent colors of citron and peach pink vibrating inside.

3. Take a deep breath and focus on your heartbeat. Envision uniting your heartbeat with the beat of the universe. You will sense a pulsing sensation.

4. The pulse will pull you inside the portal where the Great Being is waiting for you.

5. Stand before the Great Being and receive your gift, a name, symbol, sign, colors, sensations, etc. Ask your divine vocation to be downloaded to your body and being.

6. Follow the Great Being into the void to receive the Light of Eternal Union, and let the Great Being move you through the void and out the other end. The colors and sounds will pull you out of the void.

7. Once on the other side, ask the Great Being to assist you with mundane level events and issues on the Earthly plane. Ask for a personal sign and symbol to know and to feel the Great Being's presence in times of need. Wait for the sign and breathe.

8. Envision the citron and peach pink again for your return journey through the portal of light.

9. Return to your body, and repeat this exercise as frequently as you wish.

Attainment of Mastery:
The Thousand Petaled Lotus and the Disk of the Moon

Commentary: Through this meditational journey, Metatron administers healing energies to all the chakras of the body. A chakra is an energy center. Chakra means "wheel" in Sanskrit. There are seven major energy centers, or chakras, along the spinal column. These chakras are our connection to Earth and to the higher realms. As a result of many lifetimes of incarnations and of living in density and pollution, these chakras become polluted or blocked, and energy can no longer flow through them. As a result, we lose our connection with Earth and the higher realms.

In this healing meditation, Metatron begins from the top of the head where the highest spiritual center, the crown chakra, resides. He then moves down to the next center, the third eye chakra, a point between the two eyebrows. This center is for activation of the visual perception of the inner realms and spiritual awakening. Next is the throat chakra, the center for communication. The heart chakra is next, at the center of the chest, and is the seat for the exchange of love. Below the heart chakra is the solar plexus, the center for power. The area around the reproductive organs, which is the center for creative force, is the sacral plexus. Finally, there is the root chakra at the base of the spine, and this is our connection to Mother Earth. Enlightenment can only happen when all these seven centers are open, vibrating pure life force energy in and out of the body. In this healing, Metatron opens these centers and purifies them in order to fully align and activate them for enlightenment.

METATRON, CHANNELED NOVEMBER 6, 2004

Beloved of my own heart, I am Metatron. Take a deep breath with me.

Become aware of your energy moving from the top of your head down to the tip of your toes. Feel yourself inside of your body. Feel your body as though you are a witness. I will now administer a healing.

OPENING OF THE CROWN CHAKRA

We will start from the top of your head and move down chakra by chakra. At the top of your head become aware of a lotus flower. It is called the thousand-petaled lotus of the crown chakra. Feel the energy of it. While you focus on the thousand-petaled lotus, become aware of The Presence of the energies of The Perfected Presence of the I AM THAT I AM, your own God Presence. I ask that this Presence would lodge itself inside the very center core of the thousand-petaled lotus. The energy vibration of the field of the I AM THAT I AM in the formation of a body of Light begins to descend inside of a tunnel of Light. From the Heavens above the Light descends through all the levels and realms of reality, coming downwards to lodge itself in the center of the crown chakra. Above the crown chakra inside the center of the lotus sits the disk of the moon, a sphere of golden white Light.

The emblem of a lotus with the disk of the moon inside of it is the emblem of the final attainment of Mastery. The Presence of the I AM THAT I AM — God in form — descends into it, sitting at the very top of the head. Lodging itself at the very core of the lotus, The Presence of the I AM causes the final blossoming of the thousand petals of the lotus inside the sphere of golden white Light.

The Presence of God above and God within are merging and uniting in oneness on top of your head. Bring the awareness of that essence into your consciousness and your physical body. That is the ultimate purpose of realizing the Self and of attaining God Unity (to feel the oneness between the God within and the God above).

Realizing the Self (Self-realization or enlightenment) happens when, through merging The Presence of God in Form, the I AM THAT I AM takes full control of the human being's body and being. God Unity is attained with full control, and no longer the human but the God in Form is ruling over the body, the mind, the emotions, the soul and the spirit. That is when the soul's highest purpose is served. I bring to you the vibration of this highest Light.

As you immerse yourself in the healing, you will begin to notice that your own consciousness is shifting to the wider spectrum, to the consciousness of the God Presence. It is moving back and forth, from the small self to the big Self. As you shift from one to the other, you will understand that the ultimate goal is to bridge the gap between the small self and the big Self, the ultimate purpose for incarnation. You get to know only the big Self, and you know that the small self has fully immersed itself into the big Self. Then you will tap into the universal source of all knowledge, all wisdom and all expressions of God. You will no longer feel separate from any one, any place or any thing. You will see God in everyone, every place and everything. You will know God in everyone, every place and everything. And you will be united with that God in everyone, every place and every-thing. Such moments bring me joy and happiness.

I celebrate your glory with every iota of my being. I am jubi-lant in your Light. I am celebrating your blissful, loving, Presence. I am in bliss simply in being with you. Take a deep breath with me.

OPENING OF THE THIRD EYE TO RECEIVE THE INNER GUIDANCE

I now call forth The Presence of the perfected essence of the I AM THAT I AM to move through the pillar of Light down from the crown chakra to your third eye center between your eyebrows. The Presence of the I AM THAT I AM moves the energies of the Great Self, the God Self, down into your body, moving from sahasrara (the crown) at the top of your head to the ajna center, your third eye. There resides a two-petaled lotus in the ajna center. I AM. I AM. I AM.

In the course of the next three months, your visual perception of the inner realms will become much more sensitive. Call upon The Presence of Saraswati, (Sa-ras-wa-ti) the Goddess of Knowledge and Wisdom. She will bring you the knowledge, the experience and the expression of Light and godliness through her wisdom. As you open the gates of visual perception wider, ask that your perceptive Light be connected to the energies of goddess Saraswati. What you see, you shall see through the vision of knowledge and wisdom. What you experience, you will experience through the vibration of wisdom. It is very important to open this center through the energy field of a great being whose vibration is one of wisdom.

Why is it important that you open up this center through wisdom? Because in wisdom there is discretion. In wisdom there is discipline. In wisdom there is understanding. In wisdom there is the knowledge and the experience of dismination, the ability to sift through the jumble of information and data. As the perception of so many realms of reality open up to you suddenly, it is best to receive guidance through wisdom. The female creative force brings forth wisdom and knowledge. Not knowledge that is read in books, nor knowledge that is transferred by dogma. But knowledge that is transferred only by experience and refined by your own body, mind, emotions and spirit like steel that is brandished to become stainless steel.

When you open up your ajna center through the vibration of logic and rationality, you suddenly move from your emotional body into your mental body. You are no longer opening this high frequency center from that space of the heart. You become analytical, moving to the masculine force. You become focused on details and action. The world has gone awry because we have lost our focus of the larger picture, moving into a narrow-minded perception of a reality created by density — a reality which has shifted from unity to duality as a result of opening the ajna center through the mental body and energy vibration of logic.

Now, the other end of the spectrum is opening the ajna center through the emotional body: moving from seeing things rationally to seeing things emotionally through feeling and sensing; moving through the energy of the senses rather than the energy of the mind is the other end of the spectrum. When you see the vibrational force field of events, people, places and things, you immediately go into judgment about good and bad. Your senses start categorizing it into good or bad emotions. "I feel good about this, I feel bad about this. I feel not-so-good about this. I feel not-so-bad about this." It becomes a game. This time, not the mind but the emotions are in control of running the game. And again, that becomes dangerous when you see what you see through the filter of emotions. And it becomes a game when the emotions are in control of you, translating what goes on in the higher realms for your consciousness.

This is why I offer you strength for the choices that you have to make. As you move through the energies of Goddess Saraswati, the wisdom of the ages will be downloaded into your body, your mind, your emotions, your soul and your spirit. And your soul will be able to bring greater wisdom from all the four corners of the universe into your body and beingness. As a result of the anchoring of these force fields, your wisdom can then reach throughout the universe and be made available to all those that are willing and ready to receive it.

This wisdom becomes part of the consciousness of your physical grid. The physical grid becomes solidified and overlaid upon the grid system of the entire planet for the benefit of all humankind. It will eventually create a domino effect that will trigger the same understanding and wisdom in all human beings. They will be able to tap into the force field and download all the benefits from the cumulative consciousness of the grid system for themselves.

THE THROAT CHAKRA

Breathe deeply with me. I now invoke on your behalf the movement of The Perfected Presence of the I AM THAT I AM down from the ajna center (the third eye) to the throat chakra where a 16-petaled lotus resides. On behalf of (*say your name*) in the name of the I AM THAT I AM, I call forth the energies of truth and Master Hilarion to bring the emerald green vibration of truth and to lodge these vibrations in the throat center. The great chakra (wheel) spins to fill itself with the energy vibration of the emerald green Ray of Truth. As the wheel begins to spin, all the words that have not been spoken and are blocking the passageway are released. Also, the words that have been spoken in vain and in untruth are now released.

All that remains are the words that are spoken in truth and in wisdom — the wisdom that comes from the higher realms — through the grace and blessing of the beloved Goddess Saraswati. And the truth that is spoken is imbued in the energy vibration of the Emerald Green Ray. The Truth of The I AM THAT I AM.

Breathe in this energy. And allow the healing force field of this energy to fill your throat center. I spin this chakra counter-clockwise for the release of that which no longer serves you until the entire chakra is fully ablaze with the purest vibration of emerald green. At that point it will automatically begin to spin clockwise. Breathe deeply now and pause for a moment.

THE HEART CHAKRA

Breathe deeply with me. I will now move you to the energies of the heart. I invoke The Presence of The Perfected Essence of The I AM THAT I AM to take residence in the palace of the heart. I ask for the floodgates of love to open up in the heart center and that the petals of the lotus of the heart (a twelve-petaled lotus resides in the heart chakra) will give of themselves fully and completely, that every petal of this lotus will open up and reach to receive The Presence of The I AM THAT I AM in its most perfected form in the heart.

As The Presence lodges itself onto every petal and into the central core of this beautiful lotus, I now call forth the vibration of golden pink — the energy vibration of compassion and grace. Grace coming through, embodied in golden Light. Compassion coming through, embodied in pink Light. The combined forces of the gold for grace and the pink for compassion create a golden pink, the highest feminine vibration of love presently given to your planet and to this solar system. The purpose is to clear and cleanse all the dross, the heaviness and the density in which this solar system has immersed itself.

Through the golden pink of compassion and grace the density is released, and Lightness is achieved through the heart. I spin this chakra in the love and the bliss of the I AM THAT I AM, with the vibrational force field of golden pink Light from the heartcore of the I AM THAT I AM, connected to the heartcore of the Undifferentiated Source. Take a deep breath and pause for a moment.

THE SOLAR PLEXUS

Take a deep breath with me as I invoke The Presence of the I AM THAT I AM to move down and bring its energy and essence into the wheel of the solar plexus. I Am. I Am. I Am. I Am. I Am. I now call forth The Presence of the Perfected Essence of The I AM THAT I AM to intensify through the pillar of Light from the heartcore of the Undifferentiated Source and to be received through the crown chakra. Moving down to the third eye, moving down to the throat, moving down to the heart and moving down through the heart into the solar plexus, the golden disk of the sun is placed upon the eight-petaled lotus behind the belly button. This lotus has a very large core and very large petals.

Envision the disk of the sun sitting in the heartcore of the very large lotus that is turning its face to the belly button. Looking down at your own solar plexus, you would see a huge lotus with a very large bright yellow center — the size of a music CD. It sits inside your belly. Your belly button corresponds to the center of the disk, with the petals of the lotus arranged all around it. Take a deep breath and pause for absorption of the energies, while the healing and clearing take place.

SACRAL PLEXUS

Take a deep breath with me.

We now move the focus to the area of the sacral plexus in the reproductive organs. The energy essence of the I AM THAT I AM moves into the area of the sacral plexus, the spark of creative force of God in the feminine form, the Divine Mother Goddess, is now illuminated in this area of the body. Both male and female human beings benefit from the opening of this chakra. It brings the creative forces of spirit as well as the procreative forces of Earth and humankind together in alignment.

The divine spark of the Mother Goddess appears as a bright yellow-orange-red flame inside of a clear sphere, like a clear quartz crystal ball. The Presence of the I AM THAT I AM is bringing the creative force of Mother Goddess into the sacral plexus. The Divine Mother aspect is now emanating her creative force and her procreative vibration to you, bringing to perfection the future generations of human beings. It brings forth the love that emanates from the heartcore of the Undifferentiated Source, through The Perfected Presence of the I AM THAT I AM to all.

The flame begins to emanate through the entire sphere as I begin to spin the sphere. It turns into a bright orange Light burning the dross and the fear of intimacy. That creative force comes back to Perfection, and it is no longer set aside or overruled. As the Divine Mother Goddess spreads her force of creation emanating through every cell, every molecule, every electron, every iota in the sacral plexus, we spin and spin, releasing the dross, emanating creation, emanating Light, emanating oneness, oneness with the Mother force of creation. Pause and take a deep breath to allow the energies to be absorbed.

ROOT CHAKRA

Take a deep breath with me now. I invoke The Presence of the Perfected Essence of the I AM THAT I AM to move into the area of the root chakra at the base of the spine (tailbone). In this area now I place a 24-Karat gold bullion weighing one kilo (about 2.2 pounds) that connects you to the heart of the I AM THAT I AM. This is for the transmutation of negativity from the root chakra. For release of fear and disconnectedness from many lifetimes on Earth, I bring you this 24-Karat gold bullion and the golden obsidian obelisk (a tall, pyramid-shaped, golden glass structure). Moving back into the energies of The Presence of the I AM THAT I AM, start again from the top of your head down; the crown, the third eye, the throat, the heart, the solar plexus, the sacral plexus, and now the root chakra.

Invoke The Presence of the Divine Mother Goddess as Gaia. The one kilo 24-Karat gold is now placed inside of an obelisk made of obsidian, black golden obsidian. (Obsidian is a crystalline structure made of natural glass. Volcanic gasses land at the surface and solidify as brown, black, or golden black obsidian.) The obelisk is standing upright. The golden bullion is sitting inside a coffer (box), a small treasure chest made of mahogany wood with gold leaf emblems. Symbolically the wood holds the energy of Earth. Obsidian is made of lava and holds the energy of Fire that comes from the heart of Mother Earth. The gold and the black obsidian represent the minerals which come from the heart of Mother Earth. Pause and take a deep breath as your root chakra receives these gifts of healing and comes to its Perfection. All disconnectedness is now released. The body is fully grounded in the Mother Earth energies and restored to the state of joy and Perfection.

Next we will transmute dross energies with Goddess Pele, Gaia and the goddess of the sea. I now call forth The Presence of Goddess Pele to imbue and embody the root chakra and to unite in oneness with the beloved Presence of the I AM THAT I AM. It is important that The Presence of the I AM is imbued and embodied with the Mother Earth Goddess. Gaia plays the role of mother and holds the element of Earth, while Pele holds the element of Fire. I call forth the Goddess of the Sea, the emotional body of Earth and the holder of the element of Water.

I ask the three deities to stand around the mahogany coffer which holds the gold bullion. Holding hands, they make a diamond-shaped formation with your own consciousness at your root chakra as the fourth point in that energy field. I call your own consciousness to take its position, making the fourth point in the diamond shape of an obelisk. Standing around the coffer, I hold you in the Light, and I spin this grid formation with Pele, Gaia, the goddess of the sea, and (*say your name*) around the mahogany chest inside the obelisk.

As I spin, a sphere begins to appear which emanates the colors of red and gold, the Earthly emanations (red) and the purifying vibrations (gold). The red energy representing the bloodline — the life force from Mother Earth — and the gold from the core of her pure essence. The entire coffer made of mahogany with gold leaf is now emanating and vibrating the lifeforce of Mother Earth and your own physical body. I spin this chakra to clear and transmute all lifetimes of dross and pain, to bring clarity and cleansing. New roots are established — the roots of life, the roots of Light growing into the crust of Mother Earth. Emanations and beams of golden Light move from the obelisk, emanating in every direction, above and below, to the left and right, in front, behind and within. Beaming and emanating, spreading and sensing, moving and connecting to the heartcore of Mother Earth. The Presence of the I AM THAT I AM moves into the heartcore of the planet and into the disk of the sun that shines in the heartcore of the planet. All in unison, breathing the rhythm of Light, the rhythm of life, the rhythm of togetherness.

The Presence of the I AM THAT I AM is holding its forces in the root chakra connecting to the vibration of your life force and to life in the heartcore of Mother Earth. Through this emanation of oneness, the small I and the I of the God Self unite. Fully healed and united in every chakra, you begin the journey to enlightenment. The entire beingness and the consciousness that you are — in all lifetimes, in all dimensions, in all realities, in all time and space throughout the time-space continuum — past, present and future, is now illumined with the Presence of your God Self, the I AM.

This is a great exercise for you to do, simply by starting from the top of your head and moving down through every chakra of your body to the core of Mother Earth. As you practice and repeat this exercise, you will be able to complete it in a matter of a few minutes. It is all contained in the wonder of the Light of the I AM THAT I AM. And I hold you in that Light and in that vibration. And I hold you in my own heart.

In that Light, I am Metatron. So it is. It is done. Amen.

Surrender in Obedience to the Will of God

Obedience is a word that sends tremors up everyone's back. And yet obedience is the first pillar of understanding spirituality. Obedience to the light brings you power. Think of it as the opening of a doorway to greater and better things.
"I embark on this journey knowing that I am entering
into fulfillment of my divine purpose.
And I am obedient to my divine purpose."

I ask you not to be fearful…I ask you to be powerful…I ask you to surrender your will to the will of God. I ask you to say:
In the name of the I AM THAT I AM,
I walk in the truth of God.
I walk in the Light of God.
I align my will with the will of God.
I am obedient to the divine will that God has given me.
I am surrendered to whatever lessons I will learn."

And remember, for as long as human beings shall have their own agenda, you cannot be the empty vessels to carry God's will. And sometimes in order for us to be able to carry out God's will, God will have to jostle us a little bit to allow our cup to be emptied. And then as empty vessels, that cup can be filled to the brim with the nectar of God. Right now the cup is half full, and it is filled with doubt, mistrust, and uncertainty.

Sit in meditation in any sacred place or in your own sanctuary in your home where you can have peace. And very clearly with great focus put out into the universe in the name of the I AM THAT I AM all those things that you wish to achieve. Do this with clarity of focus in surrender, and apply your own highest will in alignment with God's will. (Metatron means here that it is important to know what you want and to ask or intend to achieve it with help from the I AM THAT I AM. But also ask that your own highest will be aligned with God's will. In other words, that the ability be given through grace that our limited human will be obedient to and surrendered to the divine will. Then we will not have to live our lives in upheaval until we have given up our personal agendas that keep our cups too full. With obedience and surrender to the divine will, we shall be able to empty our cups of negative karma and obstacles and shall allow the divine will to give us everything in peace.)

Review the events in your life that led you to make the decisions you have made. Simply because by reviewing them in your own mind and your own heart, you will be able to see at which point you deviated from doing what your heart and your gut knows. And you will see the turning point when you began to apply your mental will — which is very strong — to life's situations, overcoming your core wisdom and your guidance. Let us go over it step by step. What can you remember: How can you put the pictures together so that in your own heart of hearts and in your own mind, you are clear as to at what point you gave in to your willfulness. At which point did your willfulness take over from your knowing, from your wisdom? At which point did your wisdom give way to the willfulness of your mind?

When you ask for new lessons to come into your life, when you ask for the guidance from spirit, when you ask specifically for the intercession of your guides in releasing karmic debt and transforming it into your spiritual evolution, then you must heed the guidance you receive. Otherwise you have wasted yourself and your time and energy. Furthermore, you have wasted the time and energy of your guides. You have taken energy from the fabric of the universe and directed it without distribution through the proper channels. And when you do this repeatedly, you create great karmic entanglements.

Many highly-evolved spiritual beings find themselves creating karmic entanglements and consequently returning to Earth lifetime after lifetime, repeatedly clearing their karma using the power available to them in their evolved state. Eventually these beings must take a position of responsibility and start using their power for service to the Light instead of wasting it on the wheel of karma. Since you are responsible for what you create and the universe gives back ten-fold, you must assume responsibility to reap ten times what you would have sewn.

Come to an understanding of the will as it moves you — the will that emanates from your mind and the will that moves you from your heart. Align these in surrender with the will of the I AM THAT I AM. This is your highest truth. Let this truth be your guide.

Say the above mantra over and over and become power-ful. Surrender, obedience and acceptance will bring you to your final goal. There you will find the greatest truth.

In that truth, I am your humble servant, Metatron. So it is.

Mantra for the Descent Of Paramatman Light

Commentary: Paramatman Light is the highest Light of God. Para means beyond or above. Atman is the true self or the God Self. When a soul realizes the Self and reaches enlightenment, it becomes one with the Atman. Paramatman Light is the Light of the God Self which knows no differentiation, no duality, no impurity. It is the highest Light from the highest source.

METATRON, CHANNELED JANUARY 12, 2005

Beloveds of my own heart, I am Metatron. Take a deep breath with me.

The beauty of it is that you are the light of the Paramatman. In your manifestation as physical matter inside a body, the self has forgotten its existence in spirit. The ultimate experience will be when this body of physical matter remembers that it is spirit — the spirit of the Paramatman.

The Paramatman mantra has two distinct segments. One segment is for spiritizing matter, the other is for materializing spirit (e.g., "the Light of Paramatman I AM" is spiritizing matter, and the I AM the Light of Paramatman is materializing spirit).

220

When you move to the Paramatman, then there is no differentiation between something and nothing. Then it is just pure beingness. One aspect of pure beingness has taken form and accepted duality, and the other aspect of pure beingness is sitting in the great, great silence and experiencing nothingness.

We need to purify the Earth. We need to bring the energy of clearing and cleansing back to the Earth, and the only way we can do this is to go beyond what we know as form, beyond what we know as differentiated essence of beingness. We need to take the five elements back to that pure point before they had differentiated themselves into five distinct elements — Fire, Earth, Air, Water and Ether. We want to go back to that Paramatman Light in the heartcore of the ethers where all things belong, and we want to go to these locations. I ask you to start repeating these mantras as many times a day and night as you can. Fall asleep with it. Wake up with it. Receive and embody the Paramatman Light:

In the name of the I AM THAT I AM
From the point of light within the heartcore of the
Undifferentiated Source
I declare my light on Earth. (X3)
The Light of the Paramatman I AM. (X3)
I now declare the Paramatman Light through my body
onto the Earth (X3)
I command my body to receive this Light. (X3)
I command the Earth to receive this Light. (X3)
I command this Light to enter all souls. (X3)
I command all souls to receive this Light. (X3)
The Light of the Paramatman I AM.
The Life of the Paramatman I AM.
The Love of the Paramatman I AM.

The Spirit of the Paramatman I AM.
Paramatman Light I AM.
Paramatman Life I AM.
Paramatman Love I AM.
Paramatman Spirit I AM.

Three is the number for creation. When you repeat something three times, you move the energy to its creative force. Say this mantra out loud in a commanding voice. Use it as a decree and repeat each line three times. If you do not have time to go through each line three times in one sitting, then read or say them all once, then do it again all over at a later time.

In the name of the Paramatman Light, I hold you in my own heart. I ask for the grace and power of the creation and the creative force of The Divine Mother to bless and engulf you eternity to eternity.

I am your father, Metatron. So it is. It is done. Amen.

Acknowledgements

My grateful thanks to my friend Susan Batchelder for her most loving and diligent work in preparing the manuscripts, transcriptions, editing and reviews as well as all the behind-the-scenes support and compassion which she bestows upon me and this work. To Karen Bosch of Star Quest Publishing for her enormous patience and good-heartedness regarding every situation and event. It is a pleasure working with Karen and a blessing to have the light of the Star Quest Publishing team Karen and Ronna Herman as our beacons of light. To Karen also for her formatting, editing, cover design and publishing skills which are gratefully appreciated. To Kathy Zaltash for her diligent review of the manuscript and beneficial remarks as well as proofreading. To Maryam Zaltash for her efforts in website design. To my dear friend and webmaster for Waves of Bliss website, Michael Kopel for archives and sound files of the readings and for all technical support as well as for his friendship and sound solid presence through good and not so good times.

To Shabnam Sadr of Version Photography for the exquisite cover photo. To Nooshin Safai Tavakoli for the Farsi text and interpretations of the Islamic scriptures. To Dr. John Alderson for his loving foreword. To Ben Yates for drafts of grids and drawings. To Shara Shirvani and Afsaneh Alavi for reviews. Susan Batchelder, Ben Yates, Susie Farley, Tiffany Yates, Clayton Bemis, Chris Shriebstein and Patricia Gillis for transcriptions of various discourses.

The following are people who have spread their light in my life and given of their loving service to the masters by receiving the channelings and for participation in ceremonies: Avonne Lozano, Lucille Kluckas, Christopher Kluckas and all the beloved members of the New Jersey group: Fred Teger, JoAnn Mayer, Stephanie Soules, Sue Kline, Jo DePaul, Bonnie Brien, Susan Farley, Lore Walsh, Lee Renner-Faust, Mary Maher. To my beloved friend, Katie Ramaci, and the team members of Women of Wisdom Healing and Wholeness Center.

Katie Ramaci, Joice Pribushaskas, Olga Garriga, Todd Sandstrom, Clayton Bemis, Natalie Johnson, Becka Larocque, Chris Schreibstein, Beth Saxeny, Laurie Gordon, Savatri Tack, Carol Peck, Sheree Henry, Rosalyn, Leigh Ann Larson, Shari Johnson.

To the founding members of the Foundation for the Attainment of God Unity for your volunteer work and your financial support.

To Dr. John Alderson for his all encompassing support in all manners of things and for the magic of his healing touch.

Works Cited

Bailey, Alice. *Initiations Human and Solar*. Lucias Publishing Company, 1997.

Browne, Sylvia. *Visits from Afterlife*. New American Library, Penguin Group, New York, 2004.

Burnham, Sophie. *A Book of Angels*. Ballantine Books, 1990.

Catlin, George. *Christianity and the New Age*. Share International, California, 1998.

Dawood, N.J., Translated with notes. *Koran-Penguin Classics*. Penguin Group, 1956.

Doreal. *The Emerald Tablets of Thoth the Atlantean*. Source Books, Inc., 1996-2002.

Freke, Timothy and Gandy, Peter. *The Hermetica: The Lost Wisdom of the Pharoahs*. Jeremy P. Torcher/Penguin Putnam Inc, 1997.

Guiley, Rosemary Ellen. *Encyclopedia of Angels*. 2nd ed. Checkmark Books, 2004.

Kaplan, Aryeh. *Sefer Yetzirah: The Book of Creation*. Rev. ed. Samuel Weiser, 1997.

Lewis, James R. and Evelyn Dorothy Oliver. *Angels A to Z*. Visible Ink Press, 1996.

Reynolds, Brad. *Embracing Reality: The Integral Vision of Ken Wilber. A Historical Survey and Chapter by Chapter Guide to Wilber's Major Works.* Jeremy P. Tarcher / Penguin, 2004.

Safai, Nasrin. *Gifts from Ascended Beings of Light: Prayers, Meditations, Mantras, and Journeys for Soul Growth – Gifts I.* Agapi, 2003.

Safai, Nasrin. *Gifts from the Masters of Light: Journeys into the Inner Realms of Consciousness – Gifts III.* Waves of Bliss Publishing, 2005.

Safai, Nasrin. *Gifts of Truth and Wisdom from the Masters of Light: Tools for Clearing, Release, Abundance and Empowerment – Gifts IV.* Waves of Bliss Publishing, 2005.

Sathya Sai Baba. *Sathya Sai Speaks, Vol. 1: Discourses of Bhagavan Sri Sathya Sai Baba Delivered during 1953-1960.* Sathya Sai Books and Publications Trust, 1981.

Swamini Krishnamrita Prana. *Sacred Journey.* Mata Amritanandamayi Center, CA, 2005.

Szekely, Edmond Bordeaux. *The Essence Gospel of Peace, Vol. I, II, III, IV.* International Biogenic Society, 1981.

Szekely, Edmond Bordeaux. *The Essence Science of Light, According to the Essene Gospel of Peace.* International Biogenic Society, 1986.

The Glorious Quran – Persian, English, Arabic. (Quran Majid). Entasharat Judge Romi, 1378.

Thomas, Joy. *Life is a Challenge - Meet It.* Sai Sathya Sai Books and Publications Trust. Prashanti Nilaya, 1991.

Thomas, Joy. *Life is Love - Enjoy It.* Sai Sathya Sai Books and Publications Trust. Prashanti Nilayan, 1999.

Walker, Ethan III. *The Mystic Christ.* Devi Press, Oklahoma, 2003.

Webster, Richard. *Communicating with the Archangel Michael for Guidance and Protection.* Llewellyn Publications, 2004.

Wilber, Ken. *A Brief History of Everything.* Shambhala Publications, 1996.

Wilber, Ken. *Up From Eden: A Transpersonal View of Human Evolution.* Anchor Press/Double Day, 1981.

Zargar, Dr. Karim. *Kavir-E-Kimia.* (Original work in Farsi; English translations *Desert of Alchemy, Book of Zohar),* 2003.

Organization Websites For Related Information

Critical Mass of August 2005 information:
www.WorldPuja.org

Nasrin Safai:
www.NasrinSafai.com

New Age Study of Humanity's Purpose:
http://1Spirit.com/EraOfPeace

Sai Baba:
www.SaiBaba.org

SYDA Foundation:
www.SiddhaYoga.org

What the Bleep Do We Know movie:
www.WhatTheBleep.com

Shabnam Sadr, Version Photography:
www.VersionPhotography.com

Women of Wisdom:
www.WomnWisdom.com

Star Quest Publishing:
www.StarQuestPublishing.com

Ammachi:
www.Amma.org

Mother Meera:
www.MotherMeera.org

About the Author

Since 1988, Nasrin has been an internationally known Channel of the Ascended Masters and Angelic Beings of Light. In 1999, Lord Metatron requested of Nasrin to conduct channeled life readings to aid those souls who are drawn to find their life's mission and to recall their lineage of Light.

Part of Nasrin's life's mission has been to travel extensively around the world anchoring ascension energies of Light at locations on every continent through ceremonies, sacred dances, sacred languages, mantras, prayers and invocations given by the Ascended Masters. Nasrin has been honored to channel for Lord Metatron, Lord Melchizedeck, Archangel Michael, Lord Jesus, Mother Mary, Lord Buddha, Saint Germain, Lady Quan Yin, Goddess Hecate, Goddess Athena, Red Feather, and other ascended beings of Light.

She attended Chelsea School of Art in London, received a Bachelors Degree from the University of Decorative Arts in Tehran, a Masters Degree in Environmental Planning from Nottingham University in England and did her Doctoral Studies in the role of women in the development in the third world. She has taught at Harvard University and universities and institutes of higher education around the world.

Nasrin is the CEO of the non-profit organization The Foundation for the Attainment of God Unity (FAGU), an instructional and healing foundation open to all. The foundation provides classes, workshops, books and support materials for spiritual practice. All proceeds from the sale of this book support the work of the Masters through FAGU. To place a book order, contact info@WavesOfBliss.com. For information on making a tax-deductible donation, send an email to info@WavesOfBliss.com

Other Books by Nasrin Safai

Gifts From Ascended Beings of Light: Prayers, Meditations, Mantras and Journeys for Soul Growth — Gifts I. Agapi, 2003.

Gifts from the Masters of Light: Journeys Into the Inner Realms of Consciousness – Gifts III. Waves of Bliss Publishing, 2005.

Gifts of Wisdom and Truth for the Masters of Light: Tools for Clearing, Release, Abundance and Empowerment — Gifts IV. Waves of Bliss Publishing, 2005.

Gifts From Sanat Kumara: The Planetary Logos — Gifts V. Waves of Bliss Publishing, TBA.

To purchase a book, visit www.NasrinSafai.com
or email info@wavesofbliss.com.
For information on making a tax-deductible donation, email info@wavesof bliss.com.